Painting is silent poetry and poetry spoken, painting.

~ Simonides

**Painting is poetry that is seen rather than felt,
and poetry is painting that is felt
rather than seen.**

~ Leonardo da Vinci

Also by Candice James

Short Shots 2 *(Silver Bow Publishing)* 2023
Spiritual Whispers *(Silver Bow Publishing)* 2023
Imagination's Reverie *(Silver Bow Publishing)* 2023
Atmospheres *(Silver Bow Publishing)* 2023
The Depth of the Dance *(Silver Bow Publishing)* 2023
Behind the One-Way Mirror *(Silver Bow Publishing)* 2022
The Call of the Crow *(Silver Bow Publishing)* 2021
The Path of Loneliness *(Inanna Publications)* 2020
Rithimus Aeternam *(Silver Bow Publishing)* 2019
Haiku Paintings *(Silver Bow Publishing)* 2019
The 13th Cusp *(Silver Bow Publishing)* 2018
Fhaze-ing *(Silver Bow Publishing)* 2018
The Water Poems *(Ekstasis Editions)* 2017
Short Shots *(Silver Bow Publishing)* 2016
City of Dreams *(Silver Bow Publishing)* 2016
Merging Dimensions *(Ekstasis Editions)* 2015
Colors of India *(Xpress Publications India)* 2015
Purple Haze *(Libros Libertad)* 2014
A Silence of Echoes *(Silver Bow Publishing)* 2014
Shorelines *(Silver Bow Publishing)* 2013
Ekphrasticism *(Silver Bow Publishing)* 2013
Midnight Embers *(Libros Libertad)* 2012
Bridges and Clouds *(Silver Bow Publishing)* 2011
Inner Heart, a Journey *(Silver Bow Publishing)* 2010
A Split in the Water *(Fiddlehead Poetry Books)* 1979

Ekphrasticism
painted words

Don Portelance
artist

&

Candice James
poet

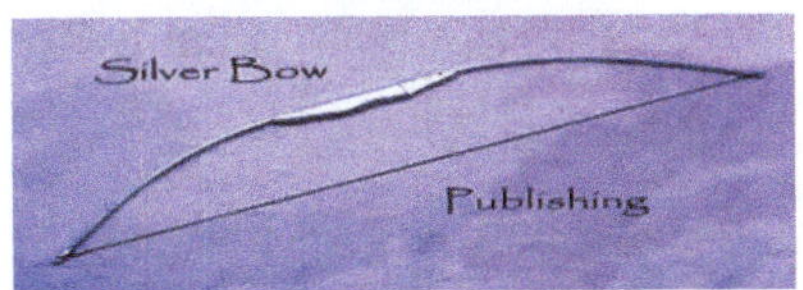

720 –Sixth Street, Box # 5
New Westminster, BC V3C 3C5
CANADA

Title:Ekprhrasticism – painted words
Cover Painting: The Dead Scrolls 'See' by Don Portelance
Cover Layout Design: Candice James
Editor: Candice James

All Artwork in the book: Don Portelance
All Poetry in the book: Candice James

4
Library and Archives Canada Cataloguing in Publication
Second Edition   ISBN 978-1-927616-11-6

Silver Bow Publishing Box 5 - 720 Sixth St., New Westminster, BC
V3L 3C5 CANADA

Email: silverbowpublishing@gmail.com
Website: http://silverbowpublishing.shawwebspace.ca

TABLE OF CONTENTS

Chronological Order of the Paintings

1960 -1969
The Nets; Kiss of the Dragon; Flamenco Fire Dance

1970 - 1979
Far City Sentries; She

1980 - 1989
Avalanche; Twilight and White Ice

1990 - 1999
Swimming Inside the Fire; Time at Glass House Mountains;
Greek Lilies; Greek Fantasy; Hillside; Yesterday's Harbour;
A Flower for Helen; Lisbon; Dark City; A Residue of Amber;
Long Houses; Short Houses; Legends of the Forest; Choir;
The Dead Scrolls "See"; The Seventh Fountain of Yang;
The Artist as a Saviour — The Saviour as an Artist; Leviathan;
A Smooth White Rabbit; Kiss at Kristopighi

2000 - 2009
Twenty-Six Forty-Four; Circle Squared' Falling Through Infinity;

Whale Song; Norfolk Windmill; Norfolk Plaza; Antique Harbour; At Rest; Cornwall Sighting; Surreal Townscape ;Flower Children; Blue Silence; Bay; Tidal Flats;The Yellow Chairs; Butterfly Effect; Winged Masquerade; Maritime Bird House; The Dream Vanished;Indian Headdress; Flower; The Empty Chairs; Don Quixote Dream; A Touch of Winter; Splash; Stairway to the Gods; At the Cabin; The Pastels; Shadow and Light; Autumn Colours; Wildflowers ;Gleaming;Timeless The Tree Whisperer; Autumn's Approach; Sweet Honeyed Dewdrops Liquid Stone; Outside, Inside; Canadians on Juno Beach; The Dream Vanished.

2010 - 2013
Sailboats and Sunsets; Breakers; The Reader; The Cool of This Blue Moment; At the Lake; Flower Fantasy Land; Crumbled to; Teapot Strangers; The Laws of the Waters; Pool of Timelessness; Splash of Red; Minnekhada Park; The Parrot; Bay of Shadows and Light; Pale Forest; Summer Dream Blazing Silence Signature

Author's Note

Ekphrasis has generally been considered to be a rhetorical device in which one medium of art tries to relate to another medium by defining and interpreting it to the audience, through its illuminative liveliness.

Through its rhetorical vividness it highlights what is happening, or what is shown and, enhances the original art, through synergy, with its description. Virtually any type of artistic medium may be the object or subject of ekphrasis. Given the right circumstances, any art may describe any other art.

In this offering of "painted words" I have taken "poetic licence" firstly with the title "Ekphrasticism". Although not a word to be found in the dictionary, it seemed the perfect word for this book of ekphrastic poetry and paintings. I have taken further poetic licence with my interpretation of the visuals presented in the paintings. The artist extraordinaire of these paintings was generous enough to also allow me to rename some of the paintings to coincide with the emotions and words that came to me while viewing them.

I thank Don Portelance for having such great and imaginative artistic talent and for allowing me the honour of writing to his paintings.

~ Candice James

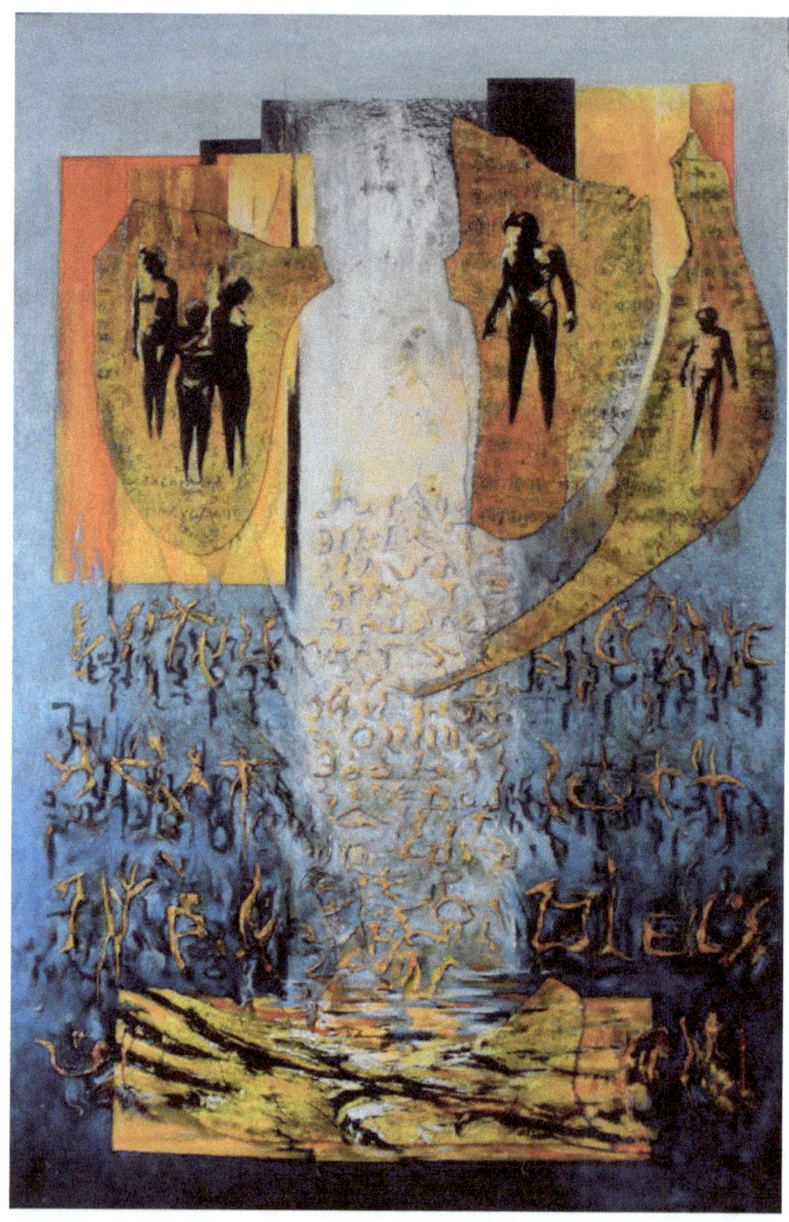

Kiss At Kristopighi

Parchments
From the past, present and future,
Inside the overflowing fountain
Of love, knowledge and wisdom,
They stand within. They stand without.

Caught in the eternal flame
Of enlightenment,
They are the hieroglyphs of the past,
The lovers of the present,
The saints of the future.

They have always been
Flowing through time,
A deep resonant symphony
Vibrating inside the tidal music of time
As they kiss at Kristopighi;
And they dance...
Oh how they dance.

They are all the words ever written,
All the music ever played
All the masterpieces ever painted,
All the dreams ever dreamed.

They are the lovers
Locked in sacred embrace,
Dancing forever together In love's eternal flame,
inside the kiss at Kristopighi.

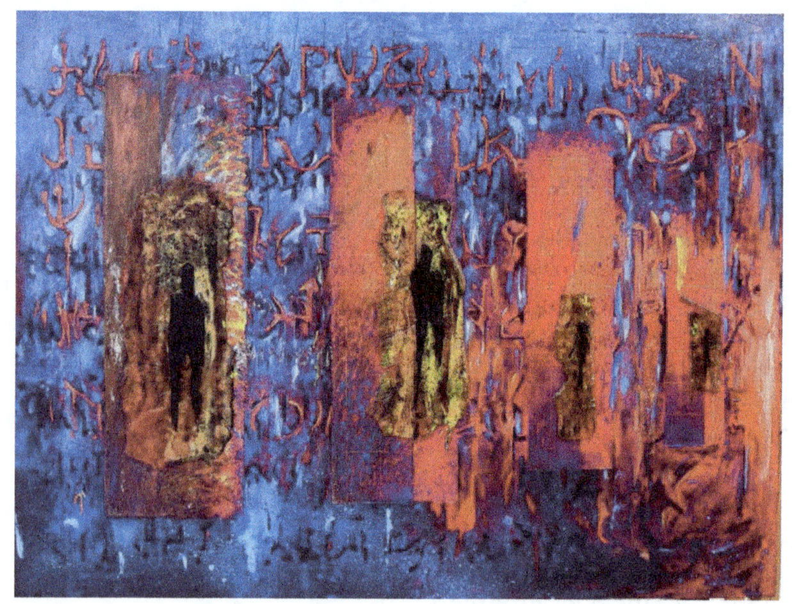

The Dead Scrolls "See"

Through the portals of timeless tides,
Visions of watery eyes
Shed teardrops onto the fabric of destiny.
Doorways haze into reality.
Invisible chains encircle my mind,
Shackle my wrists
And electrify my sleeping spirit.

The blue of a neon dream, Binding my eyes
With sunlight and ice,
Surrounds these blood red doors;
These living placentas
Tied to the womb of heaven.
I breathe the stale breath of the dead,
Mingle with the now and the living
And gaze into the future of days past.

The scrolls have eternal eyes.
They see me. They see through me,
Call my name in soft, wet whispers.
I climb into a dog-eared page
Of the Dead Sea scrolls to see.
I understand the writing
I understand the universe, the all.

A sudden divine clarity pervades
This sacrosanct atmosphere.
No longer blind, I see
What the dead scrolls see.

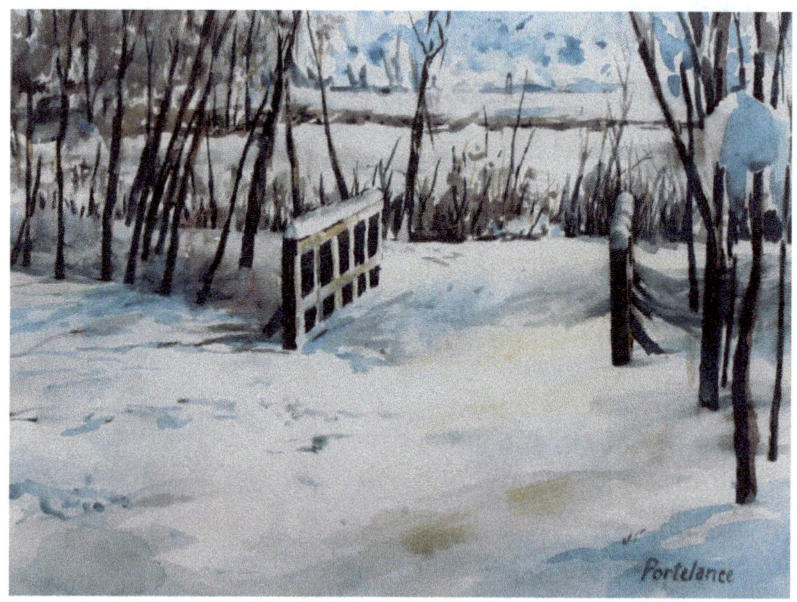

A Touch of Winter

The pristine, stark white shades of bright
Blanket the world in an icy warmth.
A film noir, reversing inside itself
In opaque ghostly images,
Rolls through a backlit sequence
Of yesterday's song and dance.
Muted memories eddy and whirl.
The white silence is deafening.

A rundown, dry-rot, wooden bridge
Creaks, heaves, moans,
Weakens beneath the weight
Of each new snowfall.
It spans the seasons with growing fragility,
Swelling and shrinking,
Flexing, weaker each year,
Toward its long time companions,
The barren trees that stand rigid,
Bound by moist, invisible freeze frames
On December's cutting room floor.

I walk inside this white loneliness,
Toward the distant mountains,
Alone with only the echoes of my mind.
I move into the mist
And blend with the sky.

I walk through this touch of winter
Untouched.

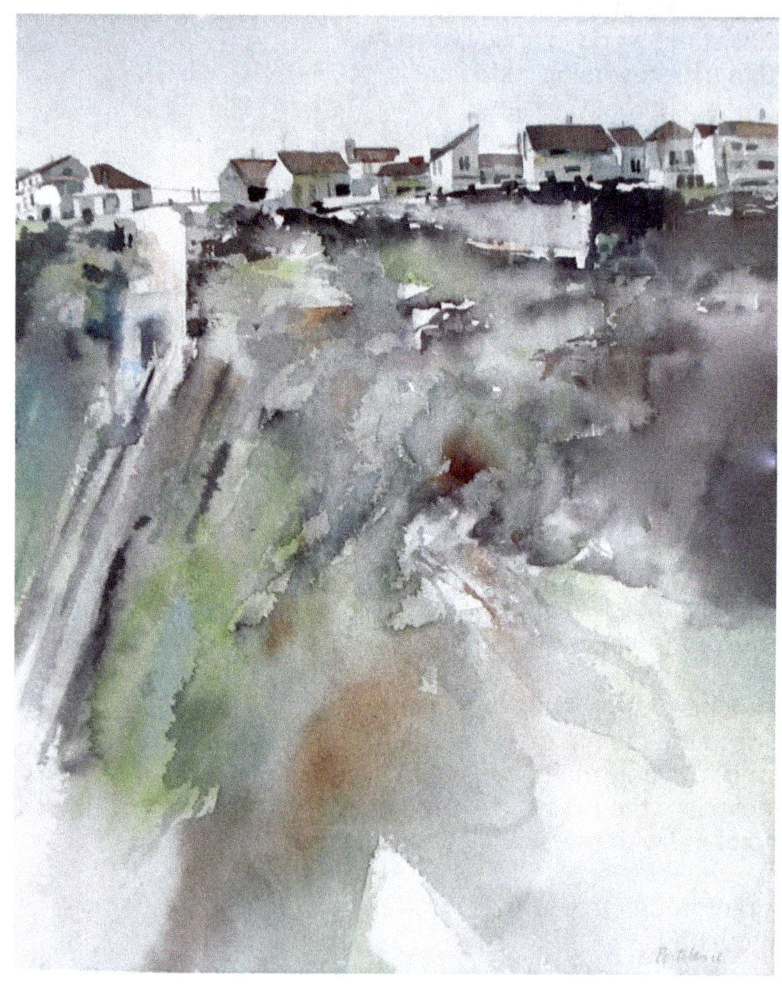

Hillside

Steep resonance,
Alive with pastoral intensity;
A kaleidoscope of emergence into divergence
Becomes more than it was, to a lesser degree.

Colours of living
Melting into each other
In a flurry of pastel images;
Hopes, dreams, aspirations and desires,
Become lost inspiration rediscovered.

Ghostly etchings
Rising up; rebellious renegades
Protesting the opaqueness they've become,
Diving into the pastel waves,
Cresting and ebbing on the vertical shore of the hillside,
Become tsunamis of thought and emotion.

Steep resonance
On the hillside;
A refrain of timeless echoes;
A constant becoming
Becoming...
Eternal.

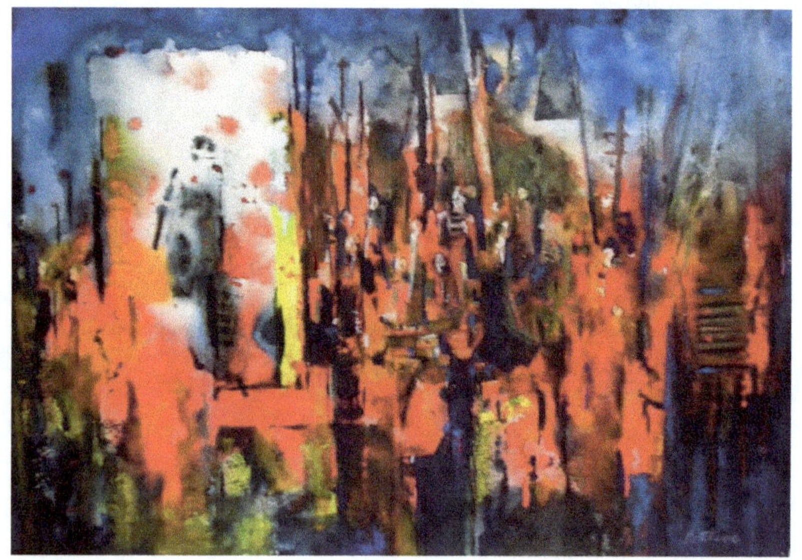

Leviathan

Standing inside the fire, Burning the edge of the wire,
Tangled, intrepid desire Rules inspiration's rebirth.

Amid the blue of a neon dream
Colours come alive, driving hard
Toward the centre of a squared white noise.
Inside God's fireplace studio,
Brushed with mystical enchantment,
The creator lifts the brush of ages,
Held by ancient sages;
Dips the brush into the living paint;
Applies it to the canvas of dreams
And a new world is born.

Climbing Jacob's ladder
To the last degree of truth,
The universe unfolds
In a blaze of colours
And bathes in the tears of heaven.

Fanning the fire,
Inspiration soars into flame.
Leviathan crumbles to ash.

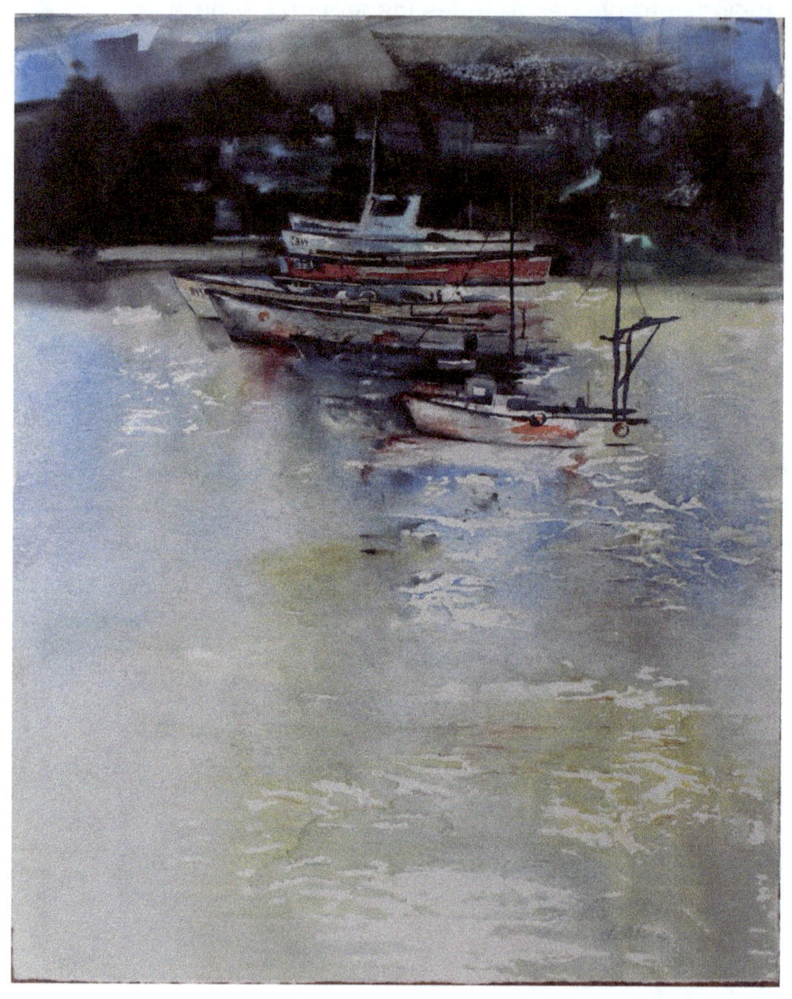

At Rest

At rest,
The boats bask lazily
In the gloss and shine of the lake.
Sparkling with the aftermath of the day
And still fresh with the electricity of the wind,
The thrill of the ride lingers on the hull's tongue.

A residue of froth and spume,
Dotting the waterline,
Slowly dissipates.

In the hush of a grooved moment,
The boats whisper and chortle
Through the thickening atmosphere,
Trading family secrets
On the slap and lap of the waves.

They gently rock in the lake's womb,
Suspended in a timeless chasm
Of motionless motion,
As fingers of darkness stretch
Across the fast dimming sky,
Palms open, gathering in
The last remnants of fading twilight,
Fist flexing, readying itself
To close the ebony curtains of night.

At rest,
In the shadows of this small infinity,
The boats submit to the elements;
To sleep,
Perchance to dream.

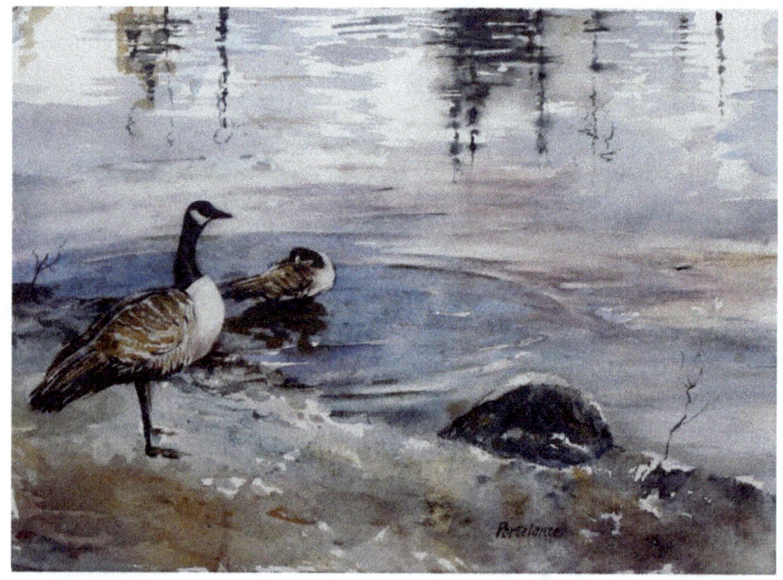

At the Lake

Upside down trees
And upright ducks
Dance on the cake of life's waters,
Reflecting the real and surreal
On ripples of glazed icing.

Viewpoints are crossroads
Into a world of dimensions
And contradictions.

Conjecture abounds
In the lap of nature's realm.

Do the birds reflect
In a world of inanimate trees?
Or do the trees reflect
In a world of animated ducks?

Molecular structure,
Atomic to subatomic,
Quark to Muon,
Quack to rustle,
To reflection, to reality
Manifest continuously
In a surrealistic universe of interchangeable
Upside down trees and upright ducks,
Becoming a compendium
Of impossibile possibilities.

The ducks wade peacefully.
The trees watch lazily.
I dimensionalize totally
At the lake.

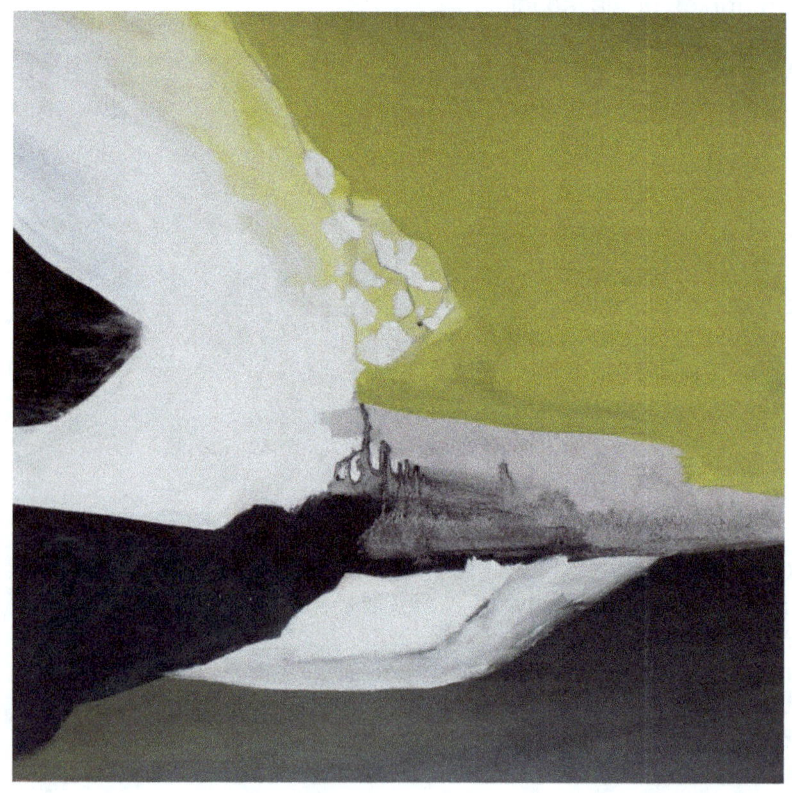

Avalanche

Up close, Industrial city,
Ghost fog and spirits' breath
Superimposed and juxtaposed
On the ediface of a shaded Grand Canyon;
All adrift atop a timeless rogue ship.
The iceburg that sunk the Titanic.

Lightning strikes
In frozen, white, jagged rods.
An avalanche filters down,
Snow dove feathers at first, floating effortlessly
Against a backlit sky of shadows.

In the distance
A Wyoming landscape fades in and out,
An extraterrestial yet familiar synchronicity
Abounding in the yin and yang
Of all things still and silent.

Gathering speed,
The ice, snow and gravel monster,
Galloping down the mountainside,
Groans with a gutteral drawl and whining moan;
A muffled siren wailing,
Through the shards of a shattered horn,
Warning of the approaching disaster.
The impending crunch and crush of white terror
Careens toward its final destination.

The avalanche roars down,
On gigantic teradactyl wings,
Opaque leather blades beating and grinding
The backlit sky of shadows into total white destruction. It screams,
at breakneck speed,
Into silence... deafening silence.

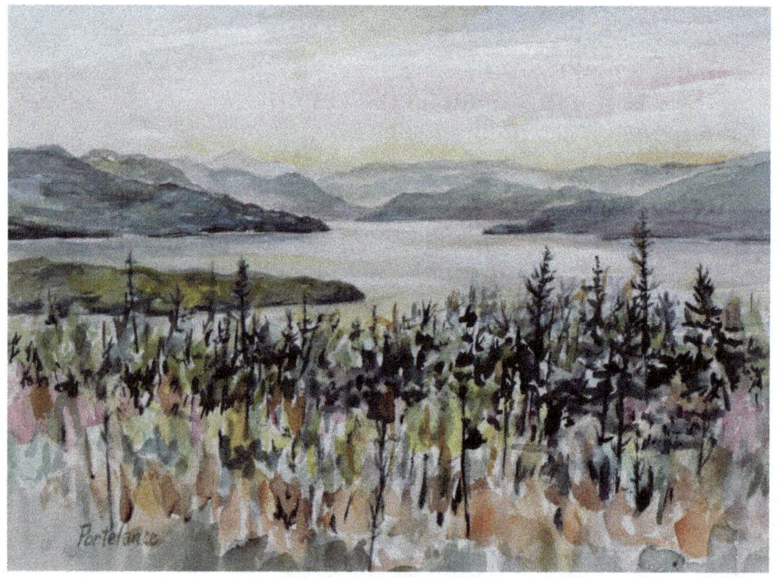

Bay

Trees and flowers, Suits and dresses
Dancing in the loft of the bay,
Keeping colourful watch,
Waiting for their ships to come in.

Earth and sky, Mountains and water
Whispering to the wind,
Keeping peaceful watch
Over the trees and flowers,
Suits and dresses
Waiting for their ships to come in.

Once there were tall ships,
Explorers and maps;
Pirates, gold and guns,
Indians and birch bark canoes.

Once these waters teemed
With hope and glory,
Brigantines and Barques,
Ponies and moccasin shoes,
Brethren of the deep,
Settlers of the shallows.

Done too soon...
So many things done too soon.

All that's left
Are the trees and flowers,
The colourful suits and dresses,
Dancing in the loft of the bay
In the infinite hold of memory's sway.

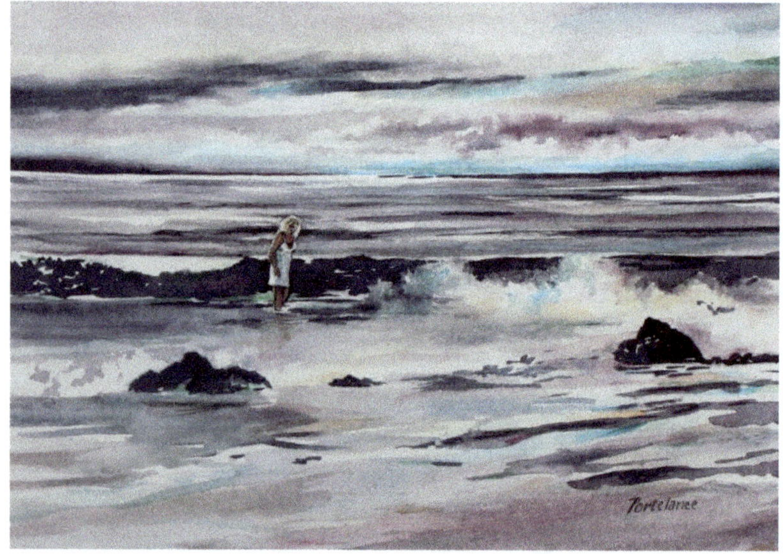

Breakers

Layered sky
On layered ocean,
A stand of rocks
And the crash of waves
Bear witness to her fluidity,
As she walks in beauty
In the shallows of the deep.

In this moment of spooled infinity
The fabric of time unravels,
Frays at the edges.
She threads effortlessly through the waves
At peace in the warm outstretched palm
Of the ocean's pastel, rainbow glove.

Alone in the backwash of the waves
She unzips a sacred azure dream.
The scent of lilac and salt
Drifts languidly on the breeze.

She wades.
She smiles,
Amid the breakers,
Beneath a slow breathing sky.

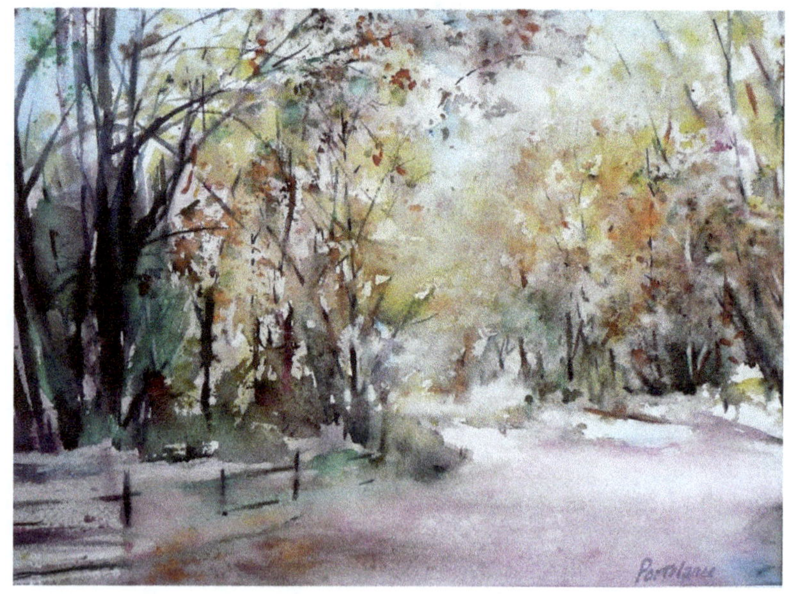

Autumn Colours

The world continues spinning around.
Seasons change without a sound
Ushering in the colours of autumn.
A cool wind whispers of things to come:
Cobalt blue skies tinged with gray,
Nature's wizardry on display,
Ready for the race and chase
As Autumn flees from Winter's embrace.

The falling away of the leaves has begun.
They've outrun their season in the sun.
Bright coloured leaves, gold, yellow and red
Tuck summer's weary face into its bed.
Under a burnished sky of rust
The summer sun turns to dust.

Tectonic seasons slipping and sliding,
The warm South wind's gone into hiding.
Raindrops bump and grind in the breeze.
Hypnotized by Fall's strip tease
Nature quickens her pulse and pace.
Autumn burns out in a fiery blaze.
Leaves disappear without a trace
As Autumn falls into Winter's embrace.

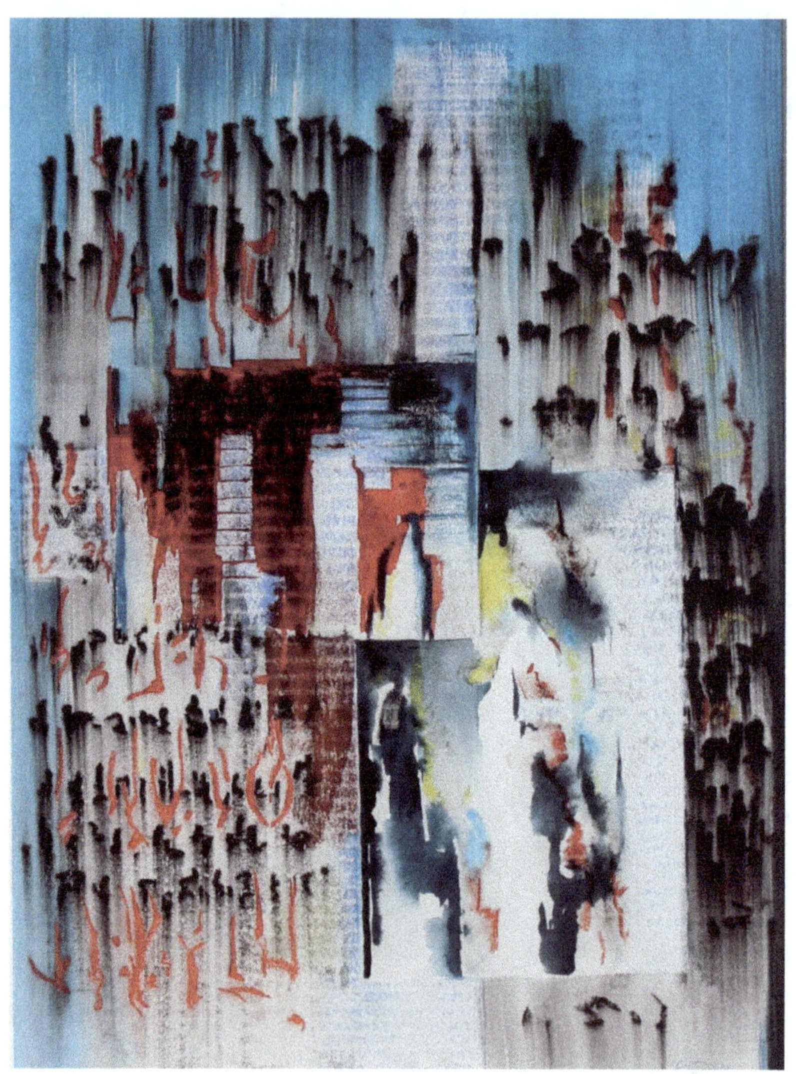

Choir

A bruised heartbeat turns into tones.
Vibrating, pulsating frequencies
Emanating colours, electricity,
Magnetize illusions to reality,
Silence to sound,
Whispers to voices,
Cascading upward to Nirvana,
Resting place of the pristine soul.

A slow breathing, inspired sky
Moistens its parted lips,
Puffs its smooth cheeks,
Blows sweet inspiration
Trumpeting through time to the lead in.
Fading up into crescendos of white rhapsodies
And opaque serenades,
Drifting and driving tenderly
Into the core of the choir.

In the valley of eight echoes
The choir arises and prepares,
Stirring angelic powers,
Awakening wings of glory.

Raw, red notes shimmer and shine.
White pearls glisten and gleam.
Blue diamonds underscore the music.
Black stilettos beat out the rhythm of the universe.
Thunder reigns down from the throne;
And suddenly...
The choir sings.

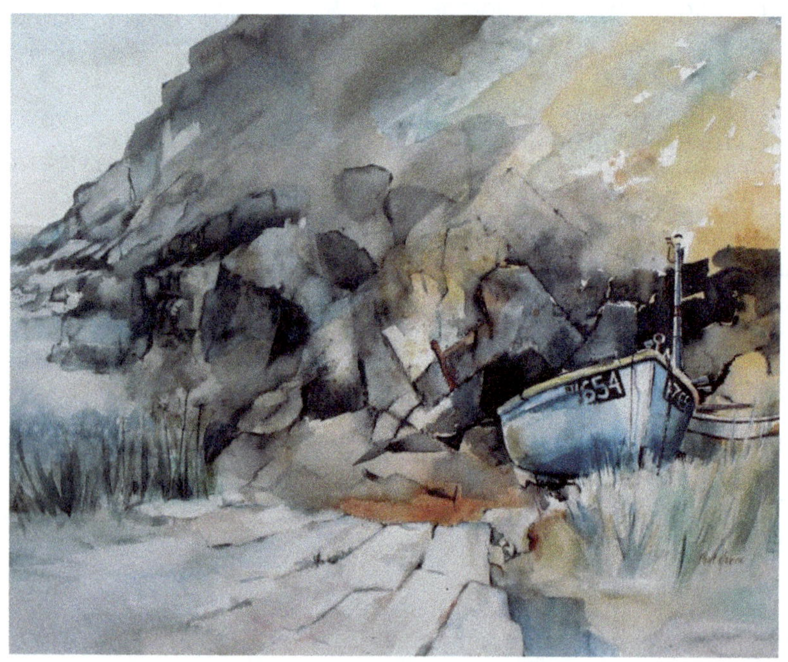

Cornwall Sighting

Steps on the dinosaur's back
Scale the shores of eternity.
Ancient ritual of the mountain,
Noah's Ark or something similar
Buried beneath turquoise and golden fleece,
Once waterlogged and dangerous,
Now landlocked in suspended time.

Bricks and old mortar,
Grass in the clay pot of the earth,
Stone igloo with a gaping maw
Muted by the tongue of time,
Battered by silent voices.

There are shadows and ghosts
Still paying tribute
To the dead everywhere,
Invisible to the eyes that search,
The souls that moan
For their pound of flesh to be returned.

There remains a boat in Cornwall
Hiding the secret to the number of days,
The succession to the steps,
And the key to the 'V' for victory.

Walk this path in reverence.
Be vigilant lest you miss it.

There is a sighting in Cornwall.

Twilight and White Ice

Stark essence of surreal sky,
Orcas swimming up waterfalls,
Ghost ships dancing with white ice,
The landscape is desolate.
Dipping into the water,
Ladling the current,
The waves gently rock
As twilight enshrouds the horizon.

The orcas and ice
Pass like ships in the night.
The ghosts of time
Click through the whirl of wind.
The swirl of tide
Slices into the battle scars
Of the jagged, juxtaposed land.

Distant mountains and clouds
Whisper secrets and stories
To the twilight white ice
As it creaks and groans its way
Toward an ebony sea.

Twilight and white ice;
Seasoned with stardust
And pearl moonglow,
Nature's divine elixlr
Mixed by the Angels,
Stirred by the Gods
And chilled to perfection
By Mother Earth.

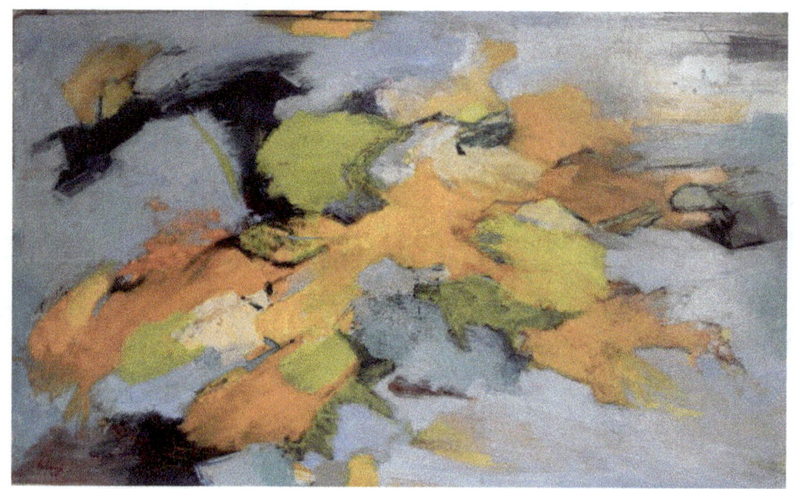

Kiss of the Dragon

A dragon's kiss reverberates
In the whispering hush
Of falling orange peels
And water-coloured sprigs of mint.

Slipping through
The rain slicked fingers
Of autumn's grainy grasp,
Leaves gather with silent applause
In this quicksilver moment
Of amazing grace.

Pale ghosts
And powder blue butterflies
Blend into the blue tent above,
Riding the tendrils of clouds
Exhaled by a slow breathing sky,
Exuding
A subtle tint of white,
A surreal hint of angels
Inside the kiss of the dragon.

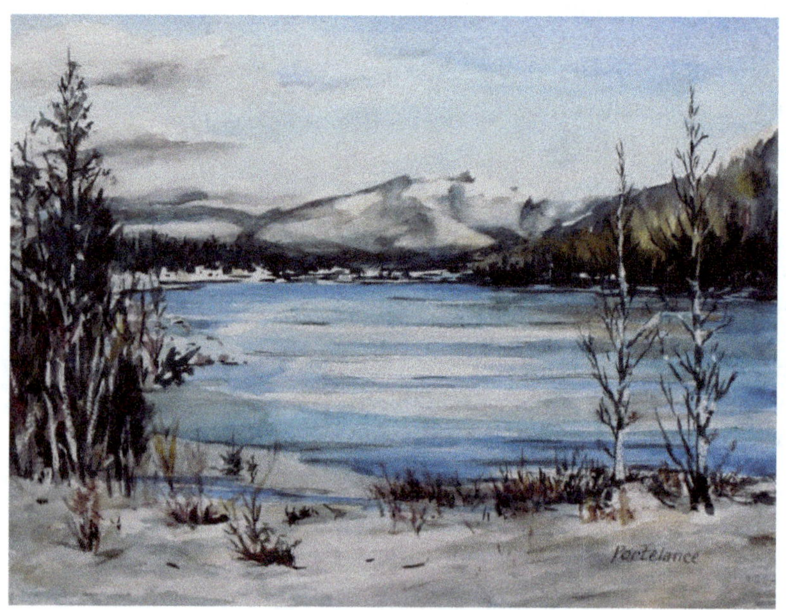

Blue Silence

In this slow grooved moment
Of powder blue silence,
The glide of nature's paintbrush,
And the whisper of the wind
Are the only sounds we hear.

At the water's edge
A cool damp creeps into our feet,
Winding itself up our legs
Like an icy ivy vine.

We rub our hands together
Thinking it may warm our legs
And hold the numbness at bay,
But the numbness continues to climb.

We begin a slow jog around the lake.
Fogged breath, blowing back in our face,
Peppers the chilled air
Making it bearable,
Almost welcome.

As we jog
The lake whispers secrets to us;
And the wind blushes our cheeks
A rosier shade of red.

We are being painted
Into nature's blue silence,
Quite unaware
That we are the artists.

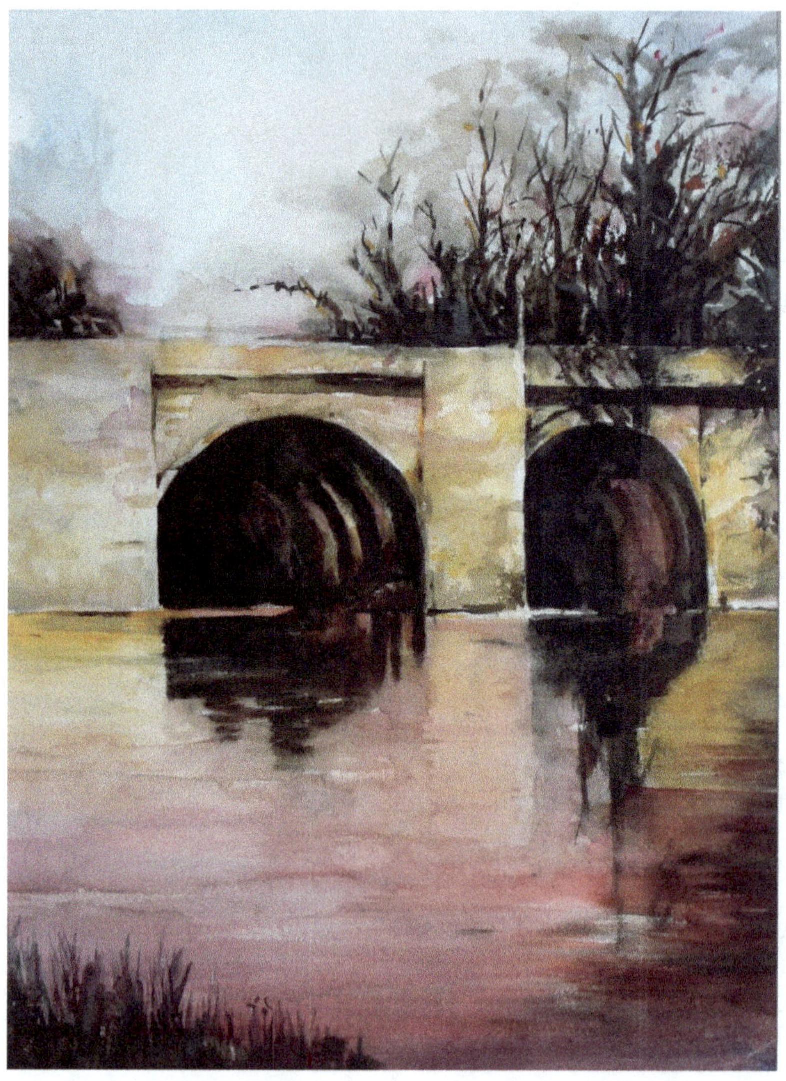

Liquid Stone

Sleeping on liquid stone,
The bridge is bathed in silence
As the grey of dusk approaches;
Emerging from the womb
Of a broken stone-age dawn.
It throbs and pulsates
With forgotten songs
And blurred melodies
Leaving imprints on the water.

On the river's pale pink sheen,
A long lost dream skates by
Losing an edge
On the wheel of time.

Awakening to a stir of echoes
This moment caves in on itself.

The liquid stone disappears
Into the dream of sleep.

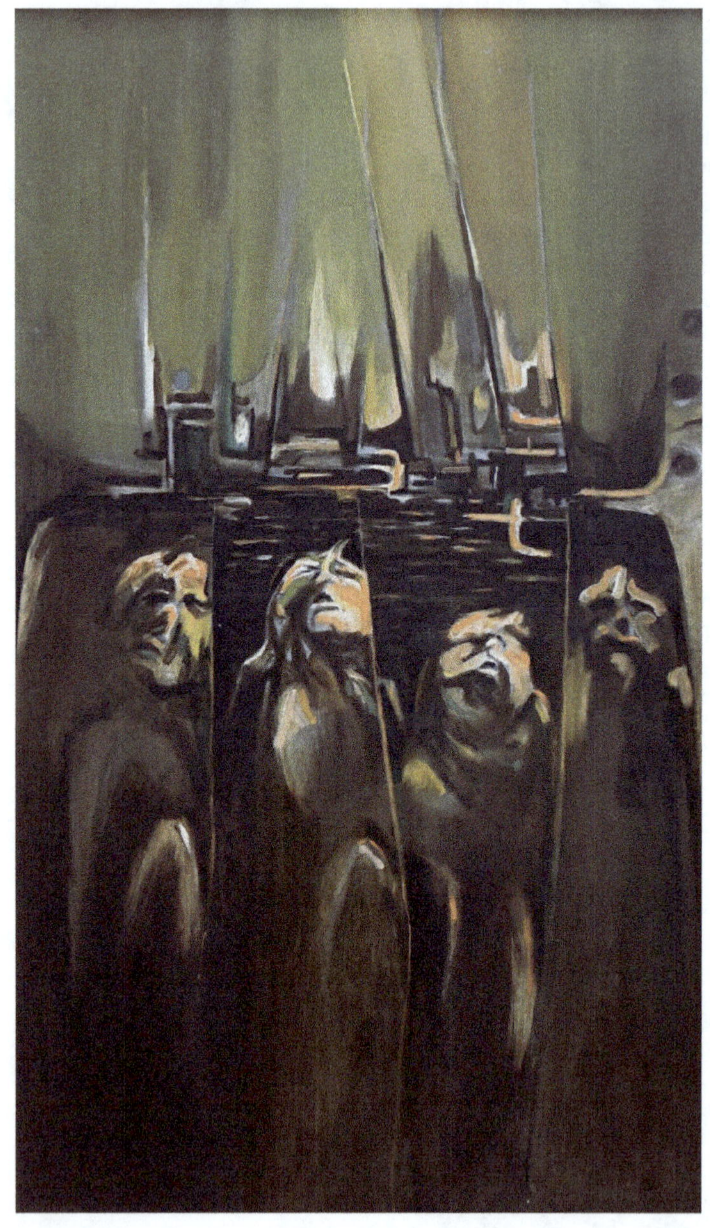

Far City Sentries

Far is near is close is not,
And they are not really there
Except in shadowy nightmares
That hide in the dark of the moon.

They are the hollow men,
The shadow entities,
A chilling moan on the wind late at night.
They are the far city sentries,
The future horsemen
Of a new and torn apocalypse.

They have evolved
Into man and machine.
Anachronistic sentinels,
Part cathedral and part prison,
They are the universal scream in the night
That nobody ever hears.

Staring like burnt out stars
Into dimly lit prison cells
They tirelessly stand on guard
For something, everything, nothing.

They have no past to seek solace in.
They have no future to run to.
They are the timeless timepieces
Rooted in the Eternal Now forever.
Lost, alone, forsaken,
Mouths twisted and torn
By strangled screams
And words they'll never speak.
They are the far city sentries.

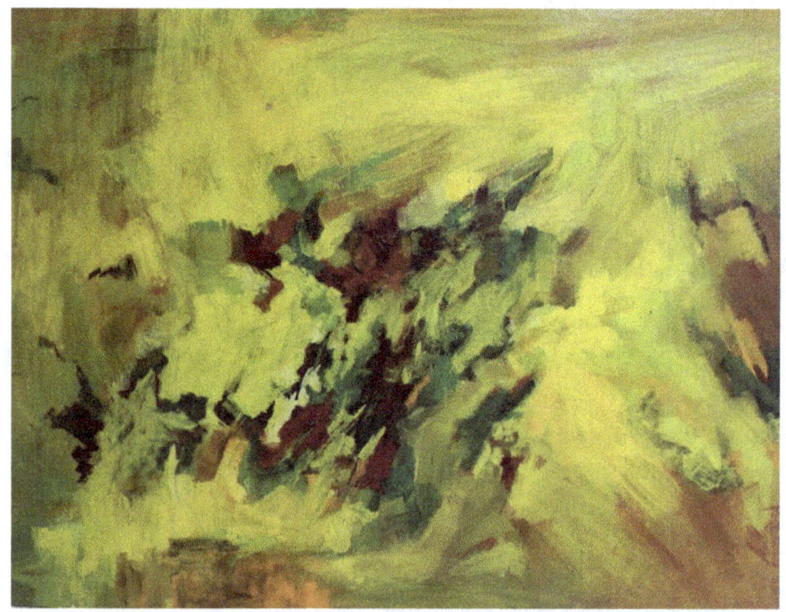

Flamenco Fire Dance

Inside the eye of the cat
Night explodes inside a blazing iris,
Teeming with colours, tones, surreal figures ...
And the dance begins.

The kaleidoscope swirl of the flame and dress,
The smacking click of boots on floor,
The whirl of the wind
In the twirl of time
Rolls in on taps and staccato waves.

A tsunami of sound,
Rhythm pounding the ground,
Hollowed out bones
Beat wet deerskin moments
To a sweet sacrificial death,
Inside the hot hurried breath
Of desire on a wire,
Stepping into the fire
Of the dance.

Dimensionalization of the flesh,
Spirit sparks and liquid lightning,
Icy hot, fiery cold,
Are bottled and sold
On the dance floor of dreams,
In the house of yellow lights,
In the eye of the cat,
In the double distilled,
Single malt heat
Of the flamenco fire dance.

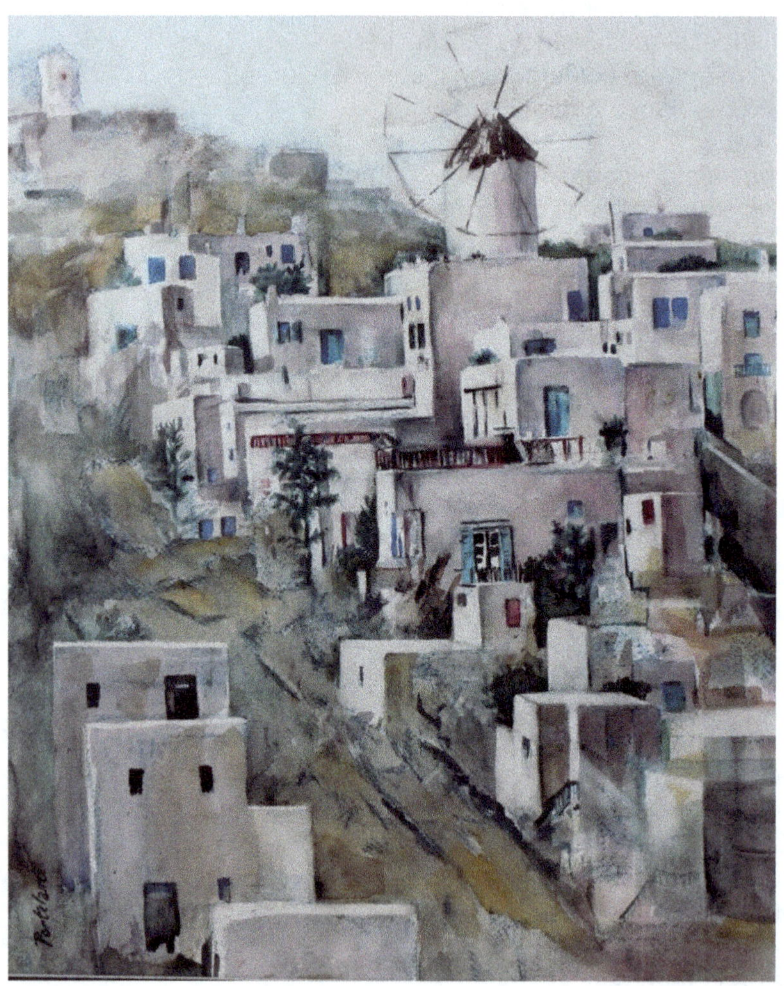

Don Quixote Dream

Climbing abstract roads
Touching spider webbed wind fragments,
Milled from the minds of artists
Still live and breath
Inside a Don Quixote dream.

In this realm
Of spectacular white silence
There are daubs of blue and gold,
Icing the fading opalescence
Of an ancient old world reverie.

The unforgiving sword of time,
In its relentless search
For new blood, bone and marrow,
Has not yet found this sacred village
Of timeless never-ending echoes.

The whisper of the windmill
Blends so magnificently
With the thick white silence
It becomes invisible
To the hands of time,
The clock of heaven
And the wheels of destiny.

The windmill turns.
The tide slows.
The town yawns,
Crawls into the Don Quixote dream
And time stands still.

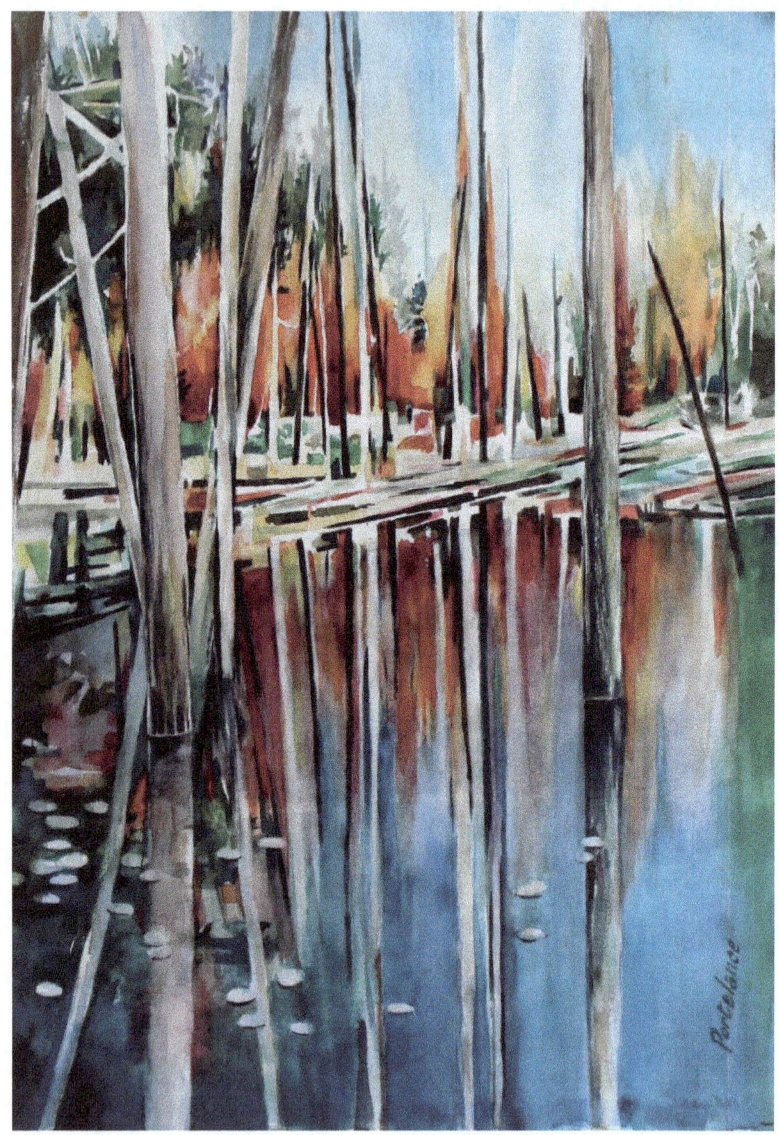

Blazing Silence

Fire and water, Sails and timbers,
White on blue
Splashed with flaming red brilliance
In a slow breathing moment
Of blazing silence.

Nature's toothpicks and dental floss
Shining the teeth of this scene
To a gleaming polish;
Boats, guide wires,
Frayed ropes and lilypads
Rippling the stir of the breeze
Through the trees;
Bearing silent witness
To the glimmer and glow
Of sundrenched, dry leaves rustling
And dancing on bowing branches
That whisper sacrosanct secrets
Into the outstretched palms
Of this solitary moment.

This solace of autumn
Is an indian summer paintbrush
Tossed in slow motion, butterfly effect
Against the sails and timbers
Cradled in the river's reflection.
It glides smoothly and instrinsically
Through the season's hallowed rush
Flexing the hush of its sable edges
Inside the satin down of nature's embrace
And the warm welcome breath
Dripping from the moist lips
Of this blazing silence.

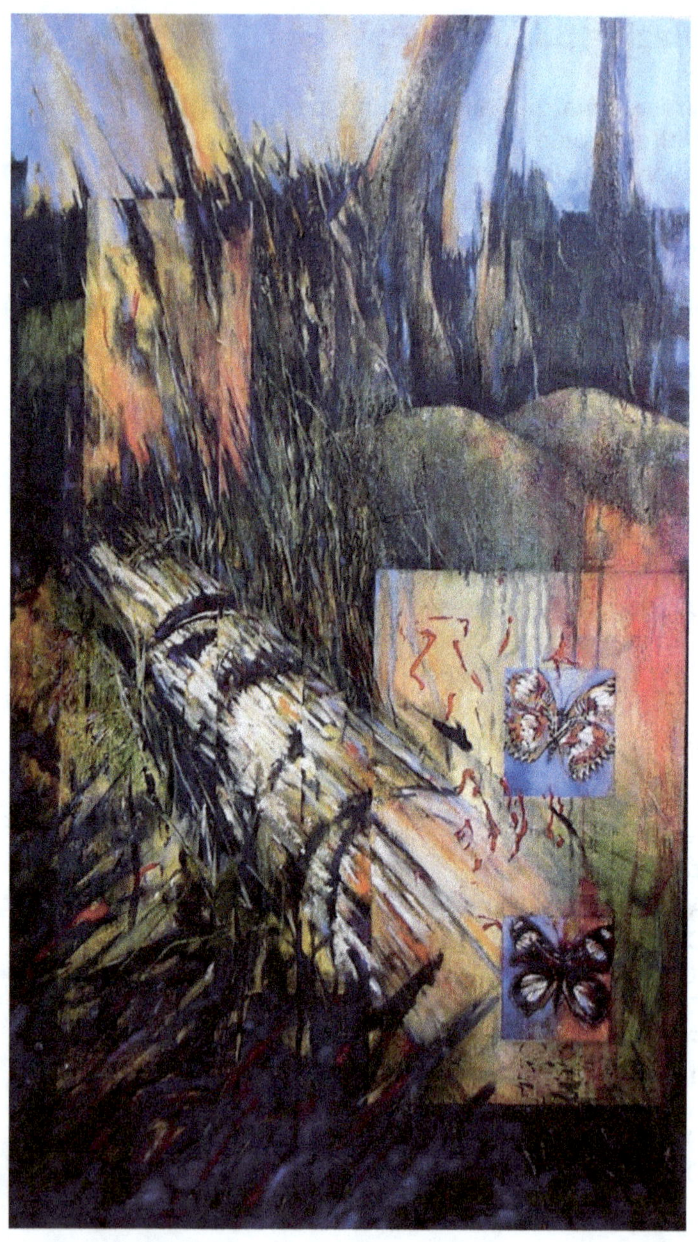

Legends of the Forest

Stone-cold, rock watchers stare,
With unflinching gaze,
Down the painted tunnels of time.

Butterflies crawl, fly and die,
Becoming specimens for amber prisons;
Silent wings never to beat again,
Locked in prismatic paradigms
In a world of broken keys.

Trees, grow, burn and fall,
Becoming charred skeletons
And cold gray vagabond ash
Tossed to the wandering winds
Scattered to the four corners of the world;
Filled with stories
Screaming inaudible whispers
Of agony and ecstasy,
Trying to explain the ever-spiralling seasons
Of Life and death.

Everything in its own time,
Everything out of sync
As worlds, times, dimensions and universes collide.
Butterflies, fire, sky, resin, ash and trees
Forever changing, returning,
In a never-ending resurrection.
There is only the Eternal Now.

The legends of the forest
And future ghosts past,
Visible and invisible,
Have become tongue-tied;
And we have become
Deafened by their silence.

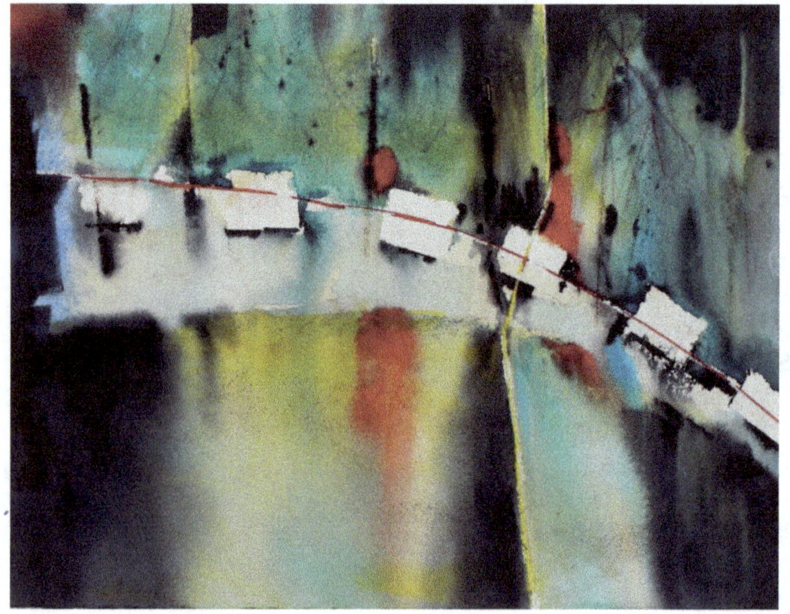

Long Houses, Short Houses

Hiawatha, Geronimo, Sitting Bull
And the ghosts of a Cherokee wind
Whisper the lost and broken legacy
Of the short houses
Through history's torn dark pages
Flayed against the shiny windows
Of the long houses.

Teepees, wigwams, tents, lean-tos,
And short houses
Scattered across the prairies,
Decorated with leather door flaps,
Tumbleweeds and sagebrush;
Deer skins and Bison hides
To warm the bones and blood
To make it through the winters.

Log cabins, ranches, mansions, castles,
And long houses
Assaulting the virginal acres,
Decorating them with towns,
Saloons and firewater;
Guns to spill the blood
That makes the roses grow
A darker shade of red.

And left behind
Is the last chieftain's head-dress
Vibrating in rainbow tones
Of fire, ice, water, earth and sky,
Transporting history's transgressions
And soiled principles
In white papered train cars
Long houses and short houses
Of dried blood and old scars.

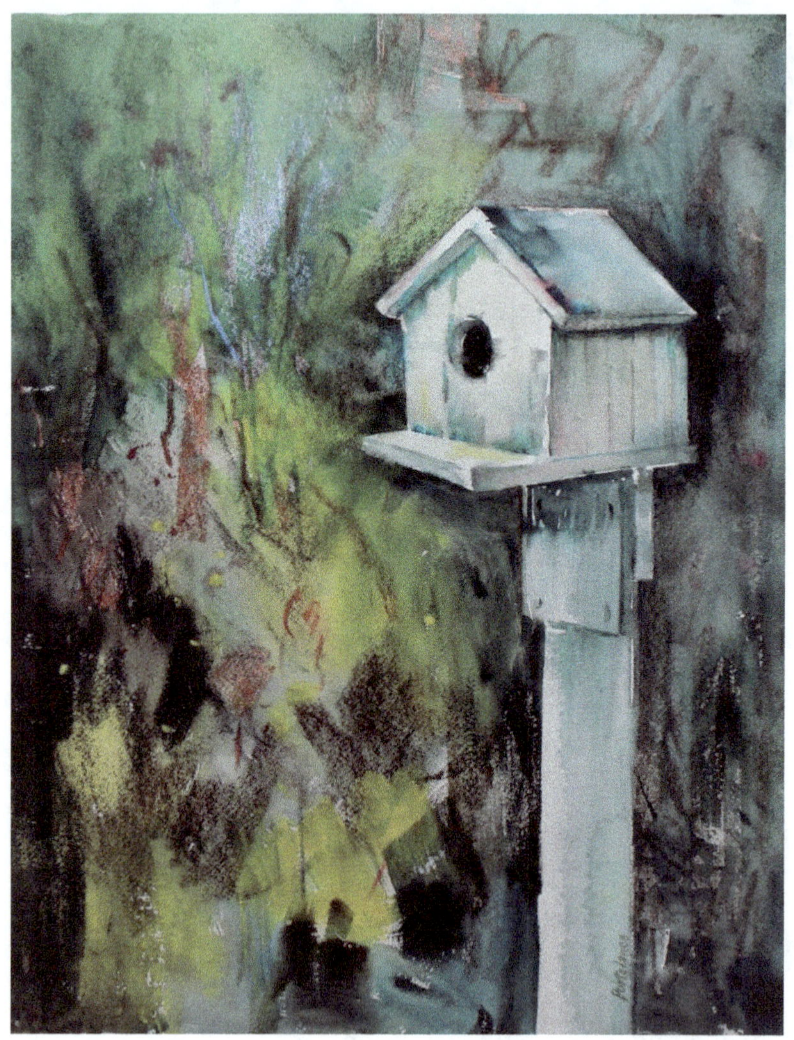

Maritime Bird House

In an overgrown backyard by the sea.
In a maritime province,
Books, butterflies, flowers, foilage,
Whispers and echoes still linger
In a maritime bird house;
The residue of past resident voices
Left behind by the absentee birds of paradise

This backyard avian condo
Is time share,
Weather permitting
And bare bones interior;
But, a luxurious feathered nest
To the weary avian traveller.

It has witnessed
Brides and grooms,
Outdoor weddings
Children playing
And old ladies rocking
In worn out rocking chairs.

It waits in silence and serenity
For the birds of paradise
To return.

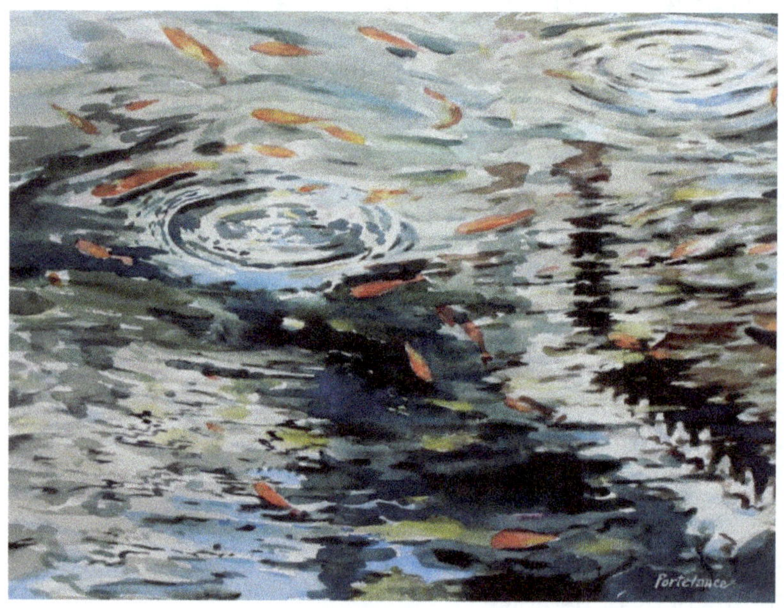

Pool of Timelessness

In a never-ending pool of timelessness,
Dreams splash and cascade
Through the ripples of time.

The orange fish,
Denizens of the shallows,
Are unharnessed ballerinas
Dancing and meandering,
Pirouetting and eddying
In pristine shiny waves.

On a layer of smooth water,
They swim into a silent ripple
And hide inside a pocket of dreams,
Alone with only the echoes
Of their movements.

Inside this moment of grooved silence,
Drawn into the mystical chant
Of a strange seductive madrigal,
They see the sky below them,
The shiny pool above.

Time reflects and ripples
On the back of a bandit breeze
And rides on a pillow of clouds
That roll noiselessly onto a distant shore.

In a moment of crystallized knowledge,
In this pool of never-ending timelessness,
In the hands of the ancient alchemist,
The orange fish
Turn to gold.

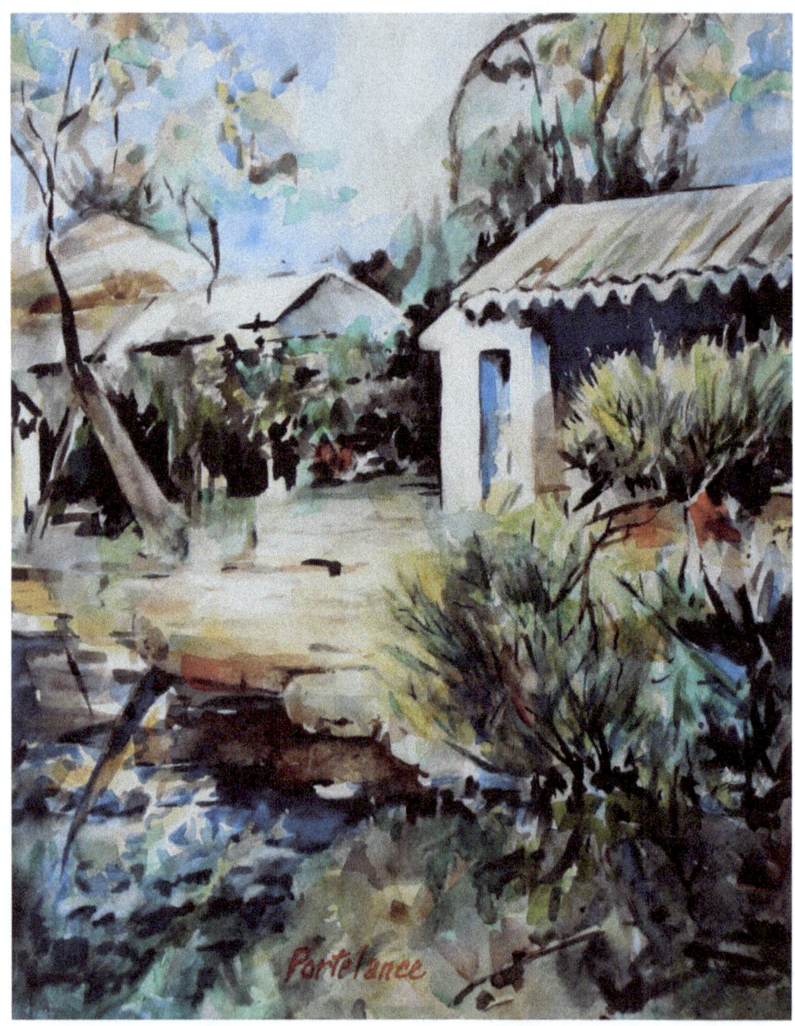

The Laws of the Waters

Flowers, bright and aromatic,
Growing from the rock bed,
Reflect the laws of the waters.
In mardi-gras disguises,
Masked as marauding intruders
They invade the wet, slick moat
Circling the slab of precipice
That supports the trees, birds,
Flowers, houses and sheds.

There is a blue door
That leads to another dimension
Of upside down apple pies
And walking birds
That have lost their wings
To their human counterparts;
Exchanging height and weight
In accordance with
The laws of the waters.

Mirrors are no longer
A reflection of the truth.

Behind the blue door
The moon is red, the sun is green,
And the sky is glistening black pearl.

A fiery fingertip
Scrawls the laws of the waters,
In luminous turquoise ink,
Onto the burnished gold essence
Of a charcoal antique stone.

Behind the blue door
There are no mirrors Only reflections.

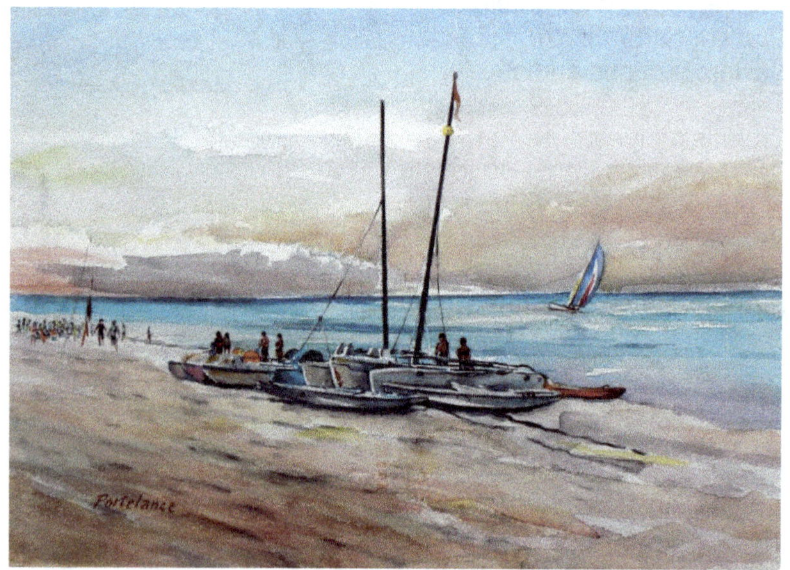

The Cool of This Blue Moment

A resonant, smooth, powdered sky,
Painted, with a day like this in mind,
Stretches as far as the eye can see,
In the cool of this blue moment.

An artist's palette, tossed against the vast sky canvas above,
Teems with pastels and abstracts, the realism of the beach;
The tanned bodies walking, frolicking;
The boast and the masts that reach to pierce
The slow moving, sparse, overhead clouds.

I gaze in awe at these balls of fluff and colour.
Formation upon non-descript formation,
Except in the top left hand quadrant
Where a mighty grey battleship
Lays at anchor peeking through the haze.

I casually play with handfuls of sand
And watch it sift through my fingers.
I spy an agate and pick it up.The promise of pale amber
Glistens inside its foggy essence.
Worn and shaped by time and tides
Into a raw, sea-sculpted, semi-precious stone,
I hold it in my hand and wonder:
How many shores has it washed onto?
How many hands has it touched?

I stand up, turn the stone over three times in my palm,
Place it in my pocket in some kind of
not quite understood ritual.
I pass by the boats, the mast, the people.
I feel the sky in my heart as I wade in the water.
The cool of this blue moment
Fills me up, and, it is enough.

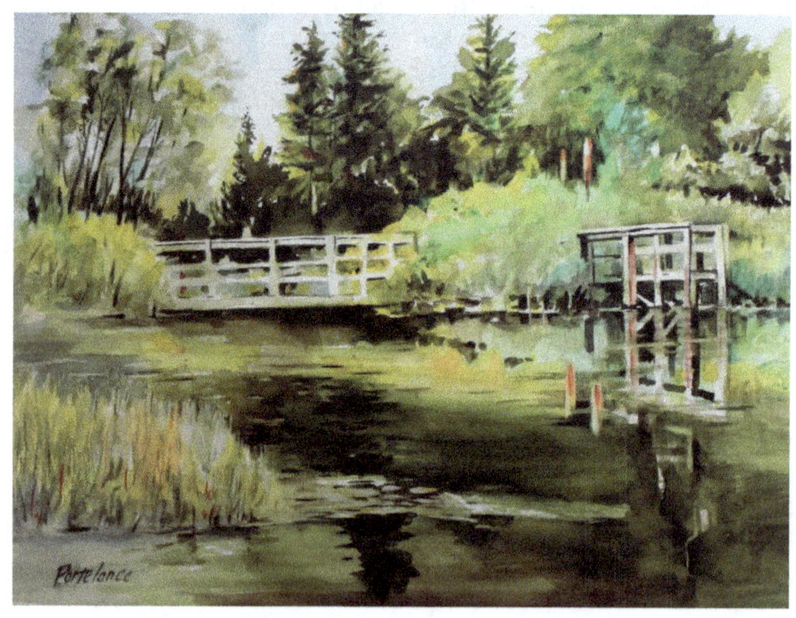

Minnekhada Park

The wind whispers kisses into the stream
As it wanders beneath the rundown wooden bridge
We once stood on at Minnekhada Park.

We stood on new ground
Bathed in sacred vows
When we hung our hearts
Higher than they ever hung before.

We wrestled the angels
For a deeper touch of love,
A stronger sense of truth,
A truer sense of magic.
It slipped through our hands like sand,
Gritty, raw, abrasive,
Scarring the new ground
Never to be new to us again.

Today the wind whispers laments into the stream
As it struggles and breaks into tears.
A fragile antique mirror,
It stumbles, trips and licks
At the slick wet wooden bridge
Our teardops still stand on.

Today, haloed in my loneliness,
I remember another day
In Minnekhada Park,
When we hung our hearts
Higher than they ever hung before,
And I realize,
We'll hang them nevermore.

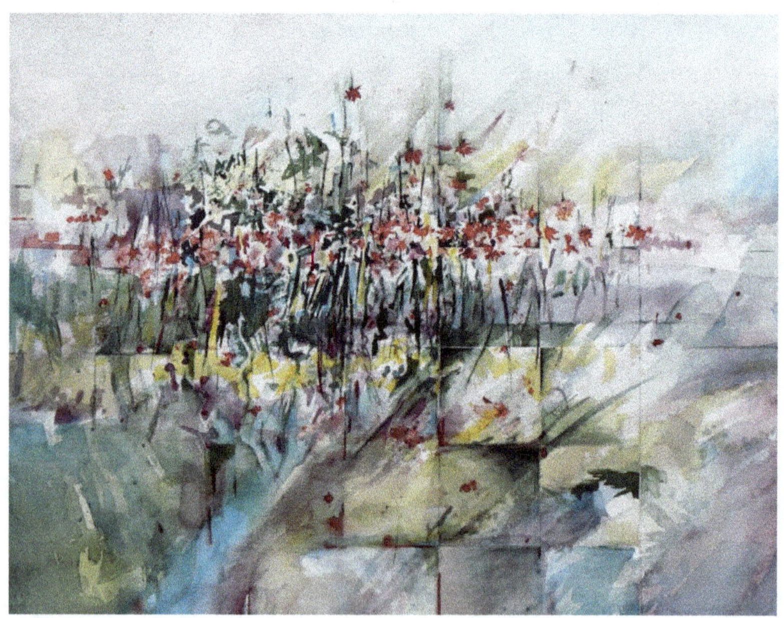

A Smooth White Rabbit

I see the colours reverse through themselves.
The moon turns inside out.
The sun burns into ebony embers
And spirals and spins in the palm of my hand.

This is a stir of coloured edges,
A field of slim fashion designer canes and walking sticks;
And beneath the overhang of swaying petals
A smooth white rabbit
Conjures up invisible magicians of light
To harvest the flowers' most precious dreams.

There are quantum worlds within the flowers.
Sub-atomic melodies and miniature dancers
Move to the beat of a different drummer,
In a different dimension
Of unknown skies and seasons,
Glass slippers, Cinderellas and Prince Charmings.

In the lush velvet underbelly
Of this pastel tranquility,
Wishes are granted and dreams come true.
Opaque plates of glass slide over each other
And etch their image and essence
Onto the pale yellow feathered ceiling
Of waxed jazz sounds of silence.

In the solace of a crimson heartbeat,
A smooth white rabbit
Pushes a shiny gold button,
Unzips the pristine dream at its core,
And the music plays a love song
Wrapped in a sacred rhapsody;
And all becomes sane in a world gone mad.

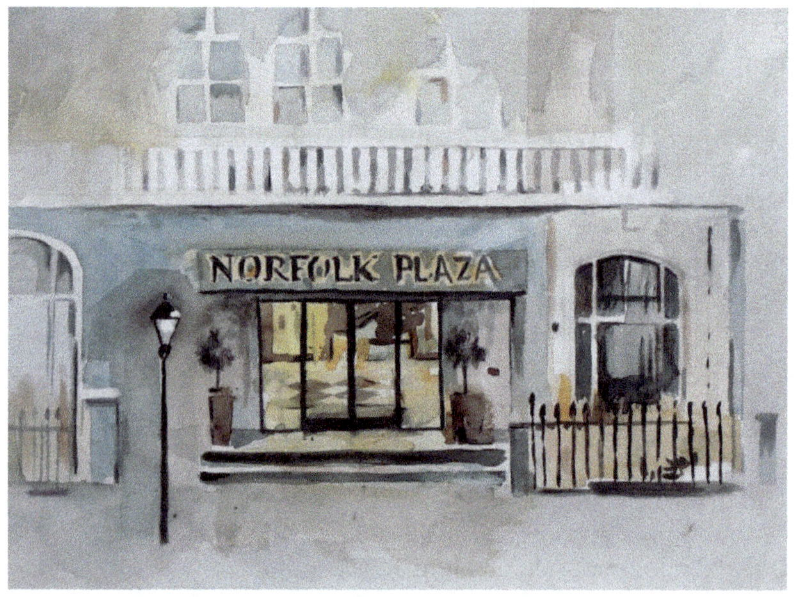
NORFOLK PLAZA

Norfolk Plaza

Beneath the streetlamp glow
Your ghost hazes in and out
In a cavalcade of smiles and tears
And never-ending memories.

The time we sang "Unforgettable"
In the plush warm drops of summer rain;
In mixed moonlight and lamp glow,
We held hands like teenagers
Innocently believing the song would never end;
We would never end.

I remember the vows we made
Under a peek-a-boo moon,
In a surreal, backlit autumn sky,
Leaning on the lamp post and each other,
Vowing the vows would keep,
Believing they would.

There was no building,
No Norfolk Plaza back then,
Just a simple suburban street
Sparsely dotted with storefronts;
And there was a wooden bus stop bench
Beside that same streetlamp.
I remember when we'd sit there
Not waiting for a bus,
Just wanting to hold each other close
And feel our souls press through our hearts.

There are some memories even time can't kill.
I loved the way we were. I always will.

Beneath the streetlamp glow
Your ghost hazes in and out.

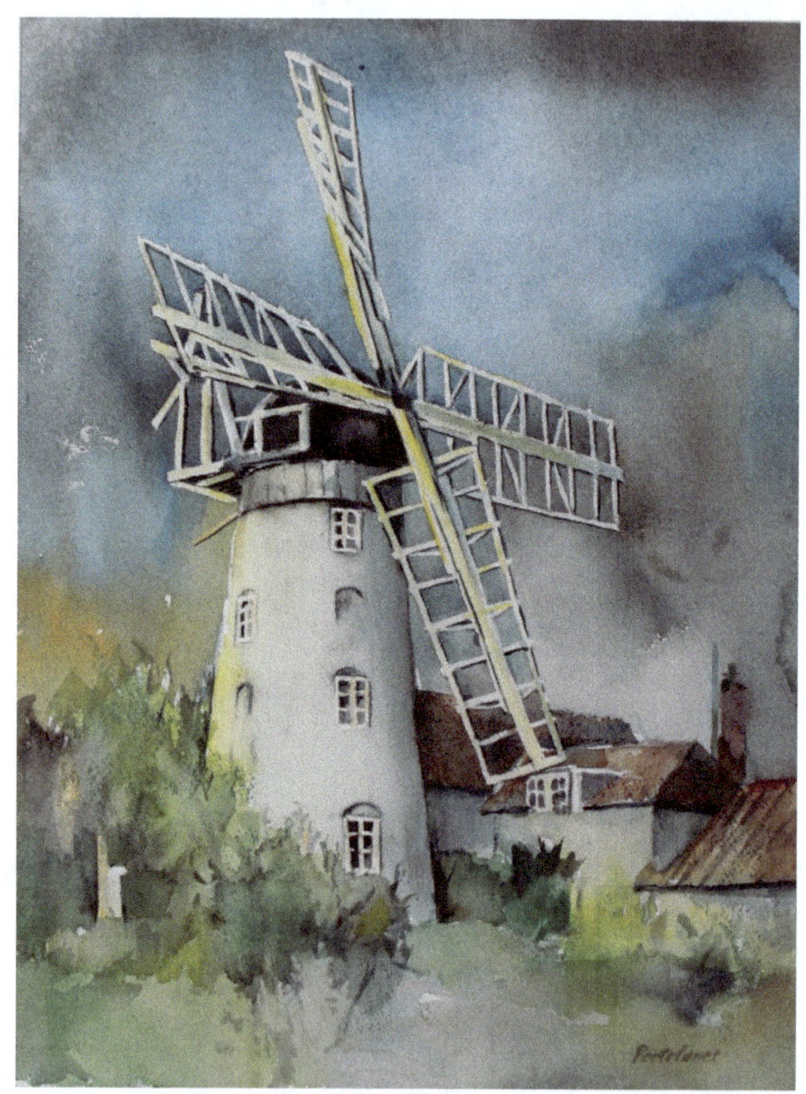

Norfolk Windmill

I still visit that old Norfolk windmill,
And I still remember
That yesterday so long ago,
Almost a lifetime ago.
So far behind, and yet,
As close to me today as two is to three.

Under a blue buttered sky
The windmill flexed its well worn wings
And rode the back of the wind
Like equestrian and steed
Racing in place, always a tie No winner.

Under that same blue buttered sky
We layed our hearts down
In the lap of the land
And the arms of love.
There was no race.
There was no winner,
Only two losers

Why do we choose to walk down roads
Better left untrod?
Why do we choose to utter prayers
Better left unanswered?
Why do circles of trust
And circles of love
Have hard jagged corners
Hidden behind doors with invisible warning signs?
And why do we stumble upon these doors
And proceed to open them?

And why, oh why do I still think of you
And visit that old Norfolk windmill?

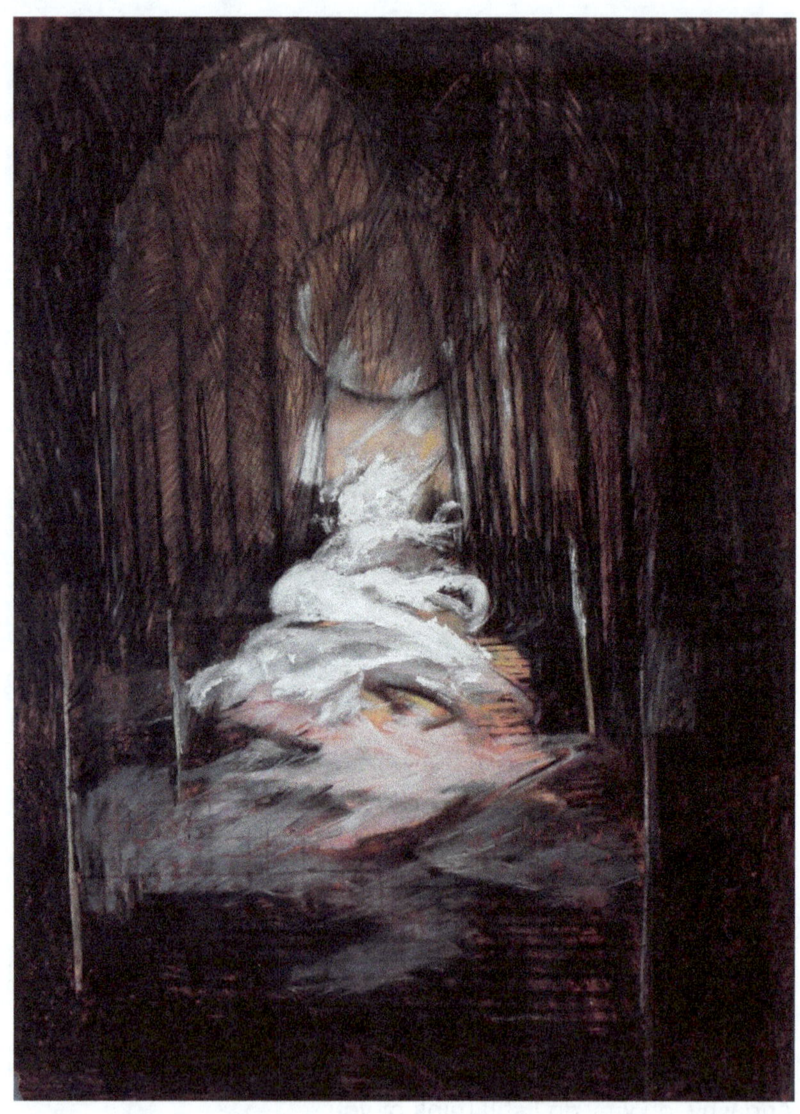

She

She lays nude
In a cradle of pastel dreams,
Wrapt in love and the river's whisper
Splashing diamonds, dampening her cheek,
Like a coveted tear.

She breathes softly
Against a pillow of satin roses,
On sheets of white velvet
Sailing on the kiss of love.
Beneath a ceiling of silver stars falling,
Enshrining her nudity in shafts of moonlight,
She becomes eternal.

She sways gently
Inside her invisible cocoon.
In a kaleidoscope dream
She rides with the wind
On the stallion of redemption
Into the eye of midnight.

She blends easily
Into her dream cocoon,
Emerging, an exquisitely painted butterfly.

She leaves her surreal world of hollowed out frailty,
Hanging by a thread;
Holding onto the fragile hope...
She'll return.

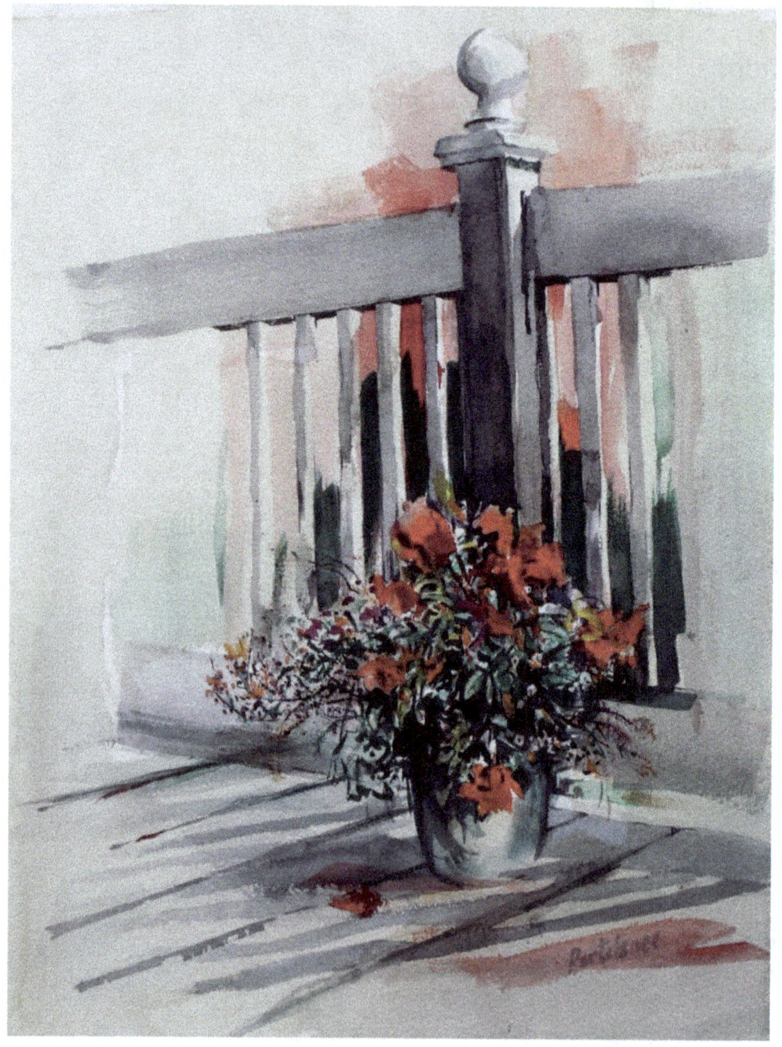

Flower Children

Within the smallest seedlings,
Eternity springs eternal
And all things come to be
That which they least seemed.

Rays of sunshine prod at thin green stems
As they poke their heads through the soil.
Mother sun draws the stems upward
With hot embrace and magnetic will,
And she smiles and sees ... It is good.

She lavishes warmth and nurtures the seeds.
The wind hears the seeds thirsty cries,
Whispers to father sky.He gathers moisture
And shapes the clouds
Into clusters of drifting reservoirs,
Filling them up until they burst,
Slaking the thirsting throats
Of his hungry crying children.

The seedling children drink voraciously,
Filling their own reservoirs,
Leaves reaching skyward
In graceful motions of gratitude.

They grow, these flower children,
Under the watchful eyes
Of mother sun and father sky.
Some become beautiful children.
Some revolt and grow into wild weeds
Putting their parents asunder,
Revering another God.

As it is in the human condition,
So it is with the ways of the flowers.

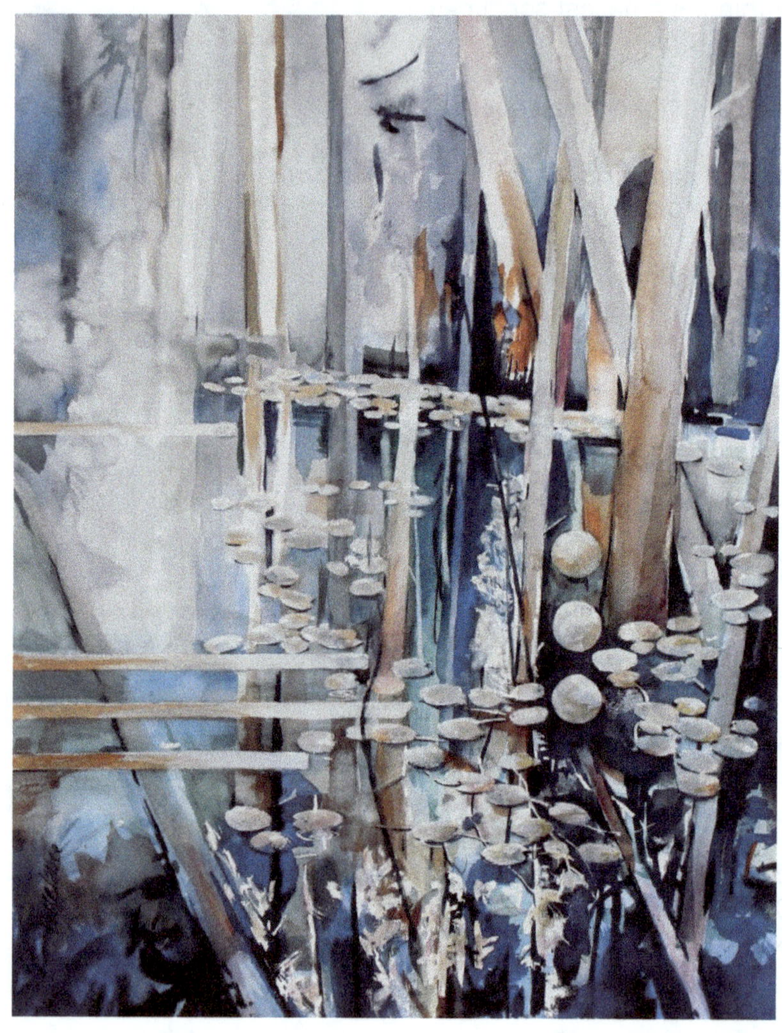

Pale Forest

An eye in the sky narrowing,
Beading down on a pale forest glade
Of watery reflections,
Measures the haphazard drift of the lily pads
In relation to the velocity of the breeze.

A jazz pianist,
Hidden in the trees at the shoreline,
Plays a burnt out torch song
For the grim reaper of love,
The dream keeper of heartache.

This corner of the world
Is home to the heartbroken,
Here and now, gone and past.
Living entities, dead ghosts,
Broken dreams, and tarnished memories
Linger in the shadows of these
Matchstick men trees.

A hazy, figurine, ghost pirouettes,
Rising in a slow swirl of mist.
The eye in the sky sheds a tear.
It lays gently on a dampened lily pad
Then slips noiselessly into the watery reflections,
Echoing like thunder,
Striking the matchstick men in the heart,
Inside the burnt out torch song
Of a pale forest lament.

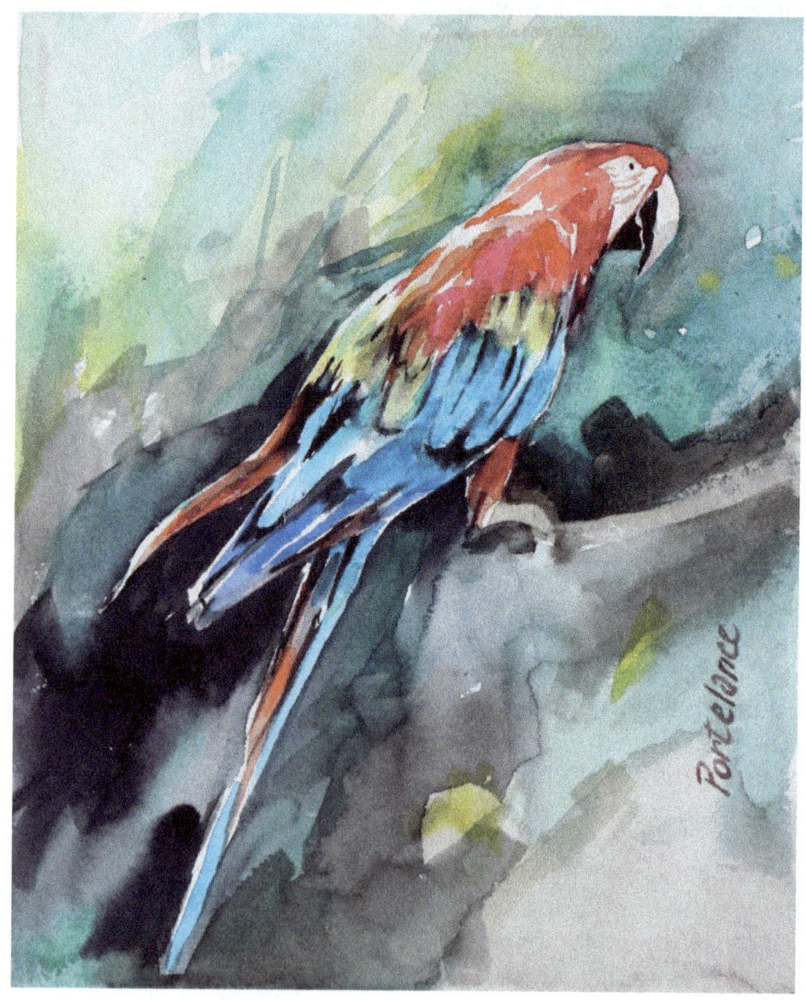
Portelance

The Parrot

On the brackish edge of a cloyed moment,
Eyes wide open asleep,
The Parrot stumbles into a nightmare
Constructed with broken toothpicks.
A barbed wire blanket of bliss
Threads its way through this dark reverie.

He dreams he sees an eagle
Hobbling across a crumbling asphalt highway,
Its soiled, broken wing
Trailing over shards of glass,
Glinting in the broken bits of moonlight
Piercing the heart of midnight.

The eagle's throat is stricken tight
Choking on unsung songs.

Guttural sounds:
      Harsh,
      Hacking,
      Piercing
            Fill the air...
Torn eloquence hung out to dry
On a blanket of barbed wire bliss.

Eyes wide open asleep. The Parrot awakens.
Ruffles his multi-coloured vivid feathers,
Bobs his head back and forth,
Sits on his perch,
Looking around for vestiges of an eagle feather,
Finds none.
Bobs his head up and down,
And squawks in contentment.

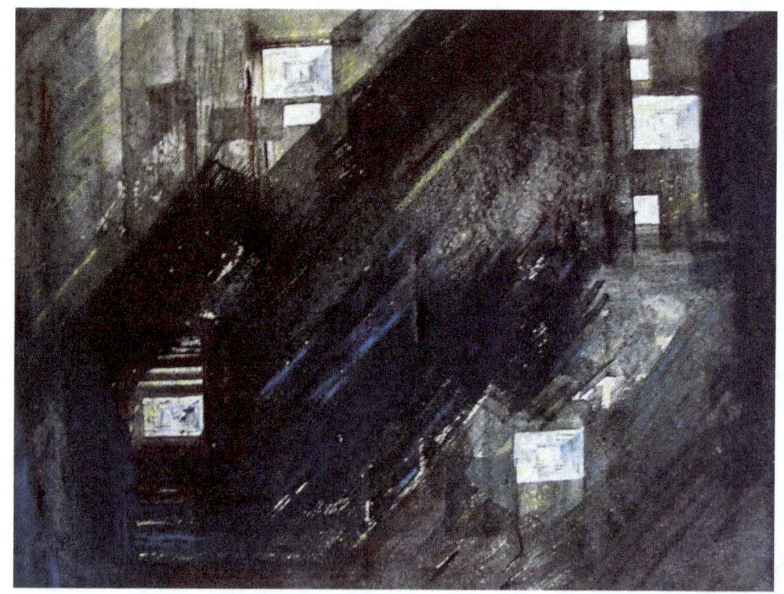

Dark City

In Dark City a lone ghost stands,
With bated breath on a deserted stage
Soliloquizing past the point of death.

Blood, dark and rancid,
Pools at the base of this nightmare.

A threatening fog hovers insidiously,
Claws, with icy slick fingers
At the raw edges
Of the city's empty voices.

An abandoned Opera House
Auditions descripted phantoms;
Some, laughing and singing,
Others, wallpaper sorrow, wailing,
Trying to pitch tears Into the folded fabric
Of a dissonant aria.

These insomniac phantoms
Fade in and out,
Like damaged neon ghosts.
Their smoky skeletons wisp silently
Through the eternal muted audience,
Feigning to touch them
With a numb caress nobody feels –
Nobody feels.

The curtain drops. The stage collapses.
A phantom tear falls
With echoing silence
In Dark City.

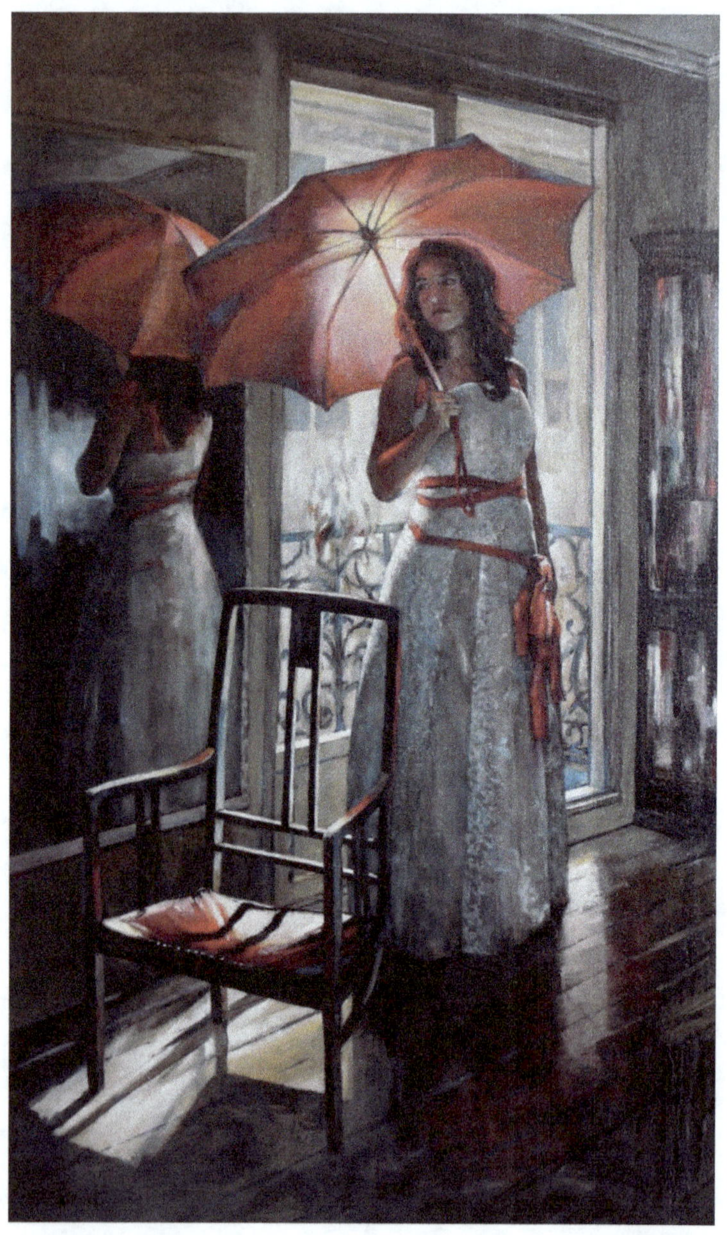

The Dream Vanished

She sat on the duvet, sewing sequins onto the frame
Of the dream she planned to wear forever;
Sparkling, shimmering,
The way her body and spirit
Shone iridescently in the mirror.

   Her eyes glazed over.
The dream hazed in and out.

She stood up, walked into the mirror
And exchanged places with her reflection.
            Encased in one way glass,
                 Slightly rippling
At the inner reaches and outer edges.
Smooth to the touch, abrasive to the soul,
The world dissolved, then re-appeared.

She stepped out of the mirror, spun around
And peered into the, now reflection-less, mirror.
She had become what she wanted to be.
Nothing, least of all herself.

She sat down on the duvet
And deftly began picking the sequins off the frame
Of the dream she'd planned to wear forever.

She put them away in her special drawer
Of useless and unrequired things,

She threw the frame into the crackling fireplace.
It flamed and flared brightly
         For a moment,
             And then...
      The dream vanished.

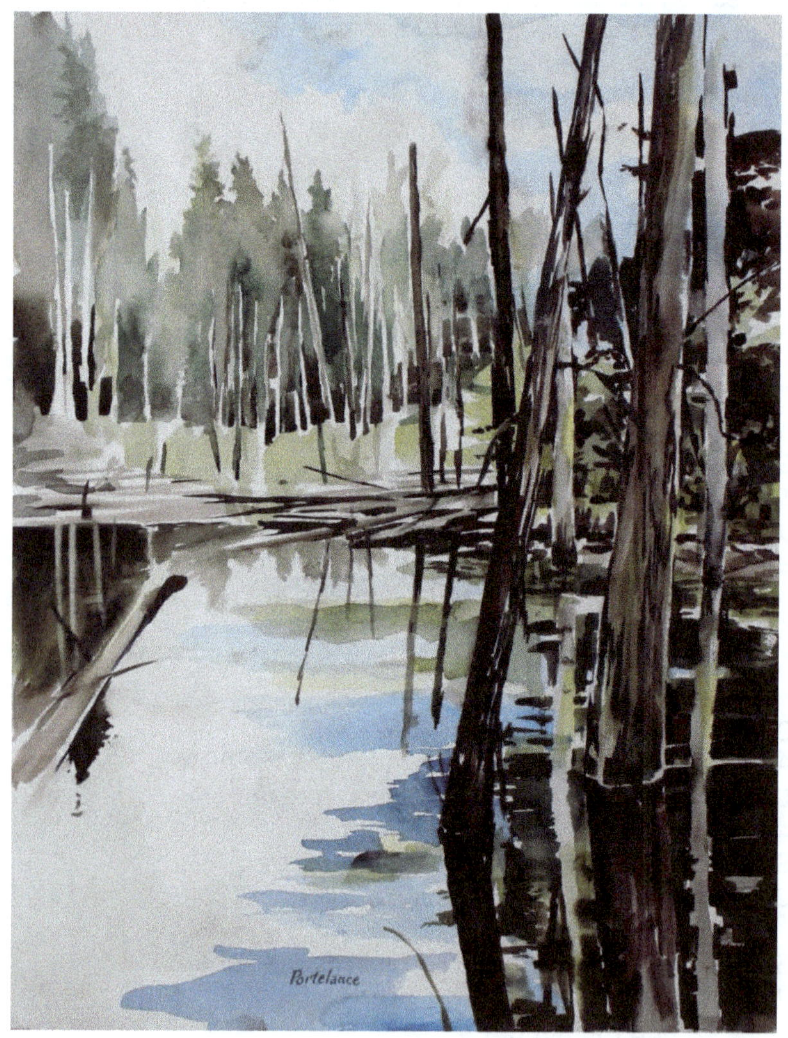

Bay of Shadows and Light

In the bay of shadows and light
The trees hold hands with their auras,
In the foggy residue
Of a slow moving moment,
The sky kneels down
To kiss the waves.

In the creek and grind of the pylons,
Somewhere behind a cloud passing by,
The high pitched keen of an eagle's cry
Echoes a mournful tone.

In the hollowed out sigh
A lost dream drifts by.
An opaque loneliness abounds
And surrounds,
Like a pale wrinkled shroud
In a castle of sacred prayer.
A whisper of voices thickens
As twilight tightens her fist
On the last remnants of daylight.

The day dissolves willingly
In the shadowy fingers of night's embrace.

In the bay of shadows and light
The trees have fallen asleep...
Fallen asleep.

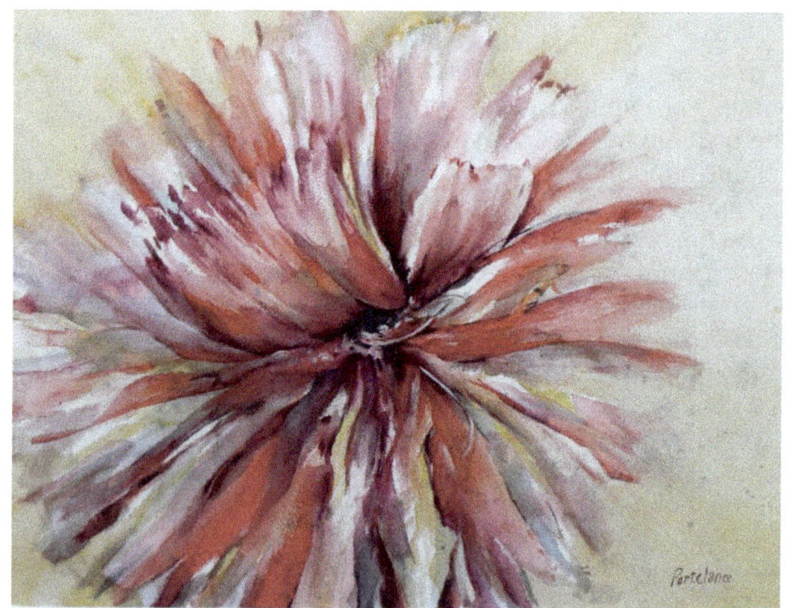

Indian Headdress

An Indian headdress,
Aburst with myriad colours,
Holds secrets and dreams in its seams,
Gives them wings
To fly through the eye of a needlepoint breeze,
Whirling, twirling, swirling,
Spiralling through itself
In a mirrored kaleidoscope
Of eternal moments.

Pungent!
A sweet aroma permeates
The cloyed atmosphere
Turning it into a sweetened elixir
To anoint the edge of the wind.

Nearby a vista looms.
Close-up a flower blooms.
Its colourful seams
Hold sacrosanct dreams.
Beauty is born for its own sake.
The proof is in the flower.

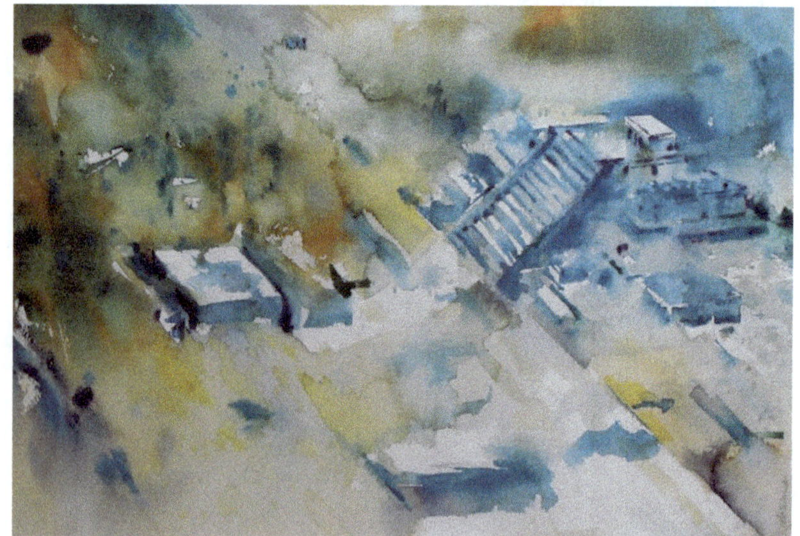

A Residue of Amber

Burnished orange embers
Still flicker on the canvas.

A pale residue of amber
Clings to the underside
Of the misty blue stairway
That leads to nowhere now.
Maps and directions are non-existent.
There is no destination here,
Just paint dropped from a golden brush
Creating a stairway to the Gods
That burns a bluer shade of amber

This amber residue stain on the soul
Vibrates with a stir of echoes
That travel the canyons of time
Relentlessly searching for the key,
To unlock the mystery,
To find the lost stairs,
To reach the stars;

To shine this residue of amber
A bluer shade of gold.

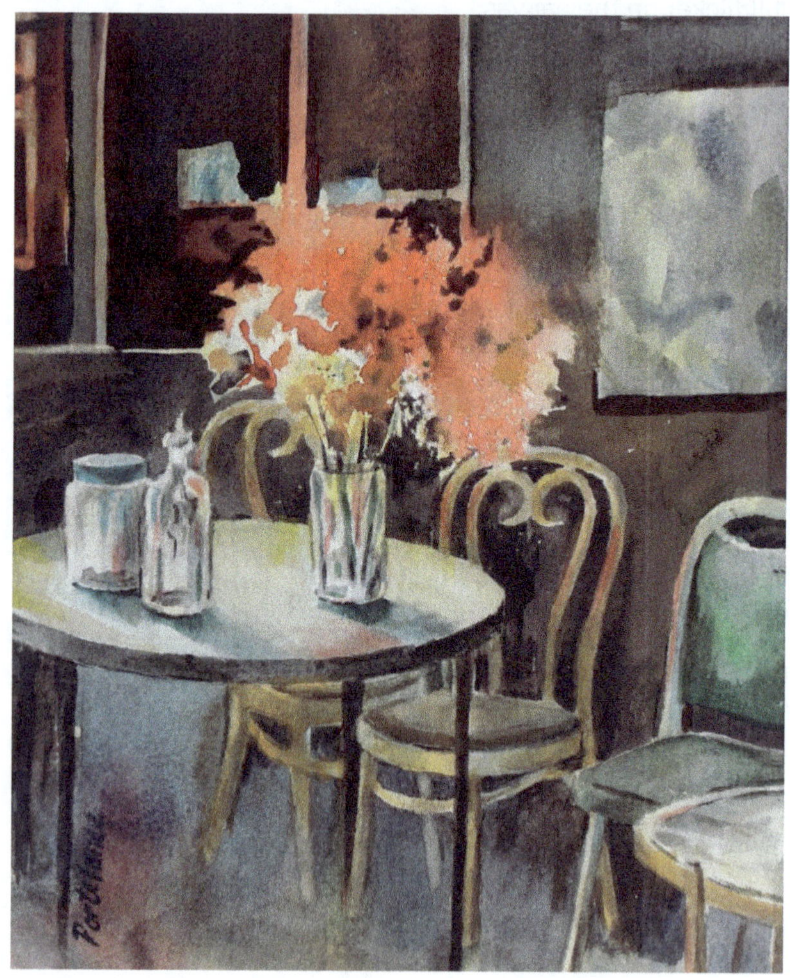

The Empty Chairs

The painting on the wall
Is dull and faded.
The chairs, where we once sat,
Are empty now.
The laughing days,
The sparkling lusty nights
Have grown dim and dissolved
Down a tunnel of time;
Empty now, like the chairs where we once sat.

Once a crystal vase
Was filled with living flowers;
A splash of bright
Against the pale painting on the wall.

Today,
The room we once sat in
Is filled with stale memories
And the dried flowers of youth.

The days of slow dancing
And reflecting in each other's eyes
Have burned out,
Like the candle glow,
Into the emptiness of the chairs
Where we once sat.

The hazy images
Of those vibrant days
Are dull and faded
Like the painting on the wall;
And my heart Is empty now,
Like the chairs where we once sat.

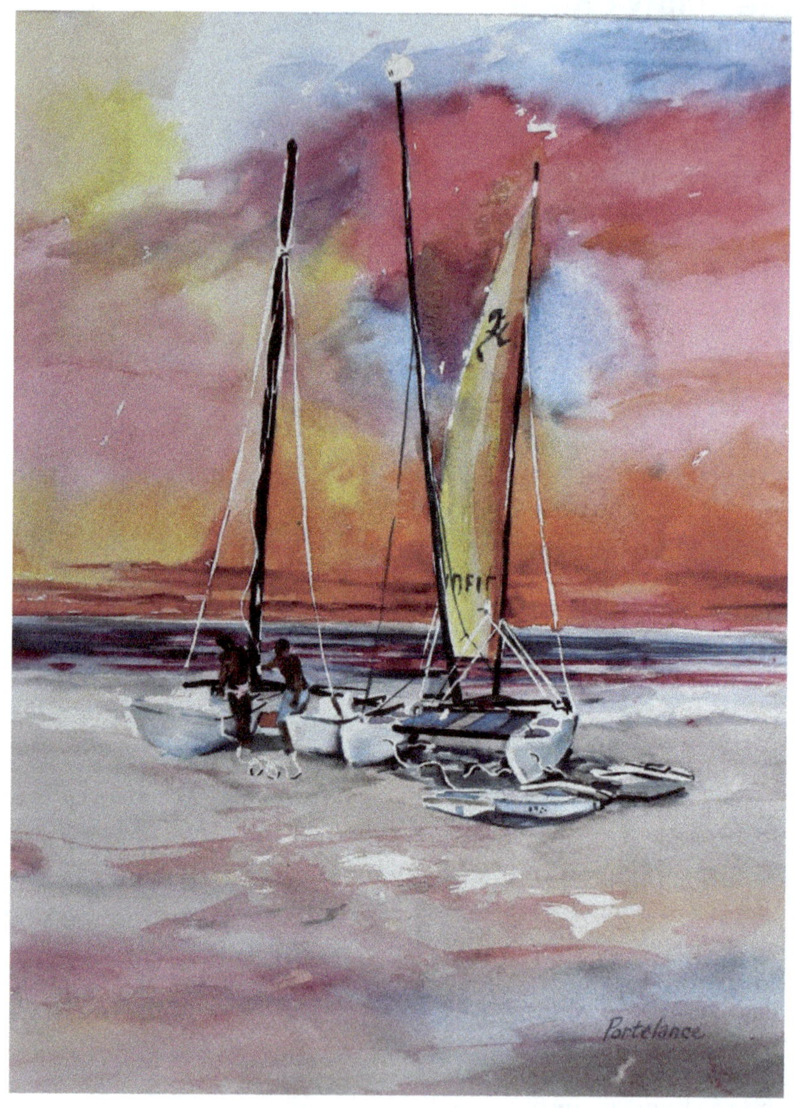

Sailboats and Sunsets

The sailboats at rest on the shore,
Backlit by a fiery sunset,
Sit in quiet reflection
On a stretch of silvered sand.

The slight remnant of wind
And hush of waves
Paint a surreal layer of solace
Onto the glistening shoreline.

The windswept hair
and sun steeped bodies of the sea captains
Gleam in the flaring fiery sunset.

Patches of bleu de France slowly dissolve
Onto twilight's thirsty tongue
And the beach becomes deserted.

The fiery sunset dims
As night flexes her greedy fingers
And squeezes the last remnants
Of sky blaze to cinders.

Looming shadows blanket the sand.
The wind slows, stills.
Darkness disrobes.

The sailboats on the shore
Slip slowly and gracefully
Into the ebony pocket of night.

The sailboats at rest on the shore,
And the fading fiery sunset,
Bow their heads and fall asleep
In the cradle of dreams to come.

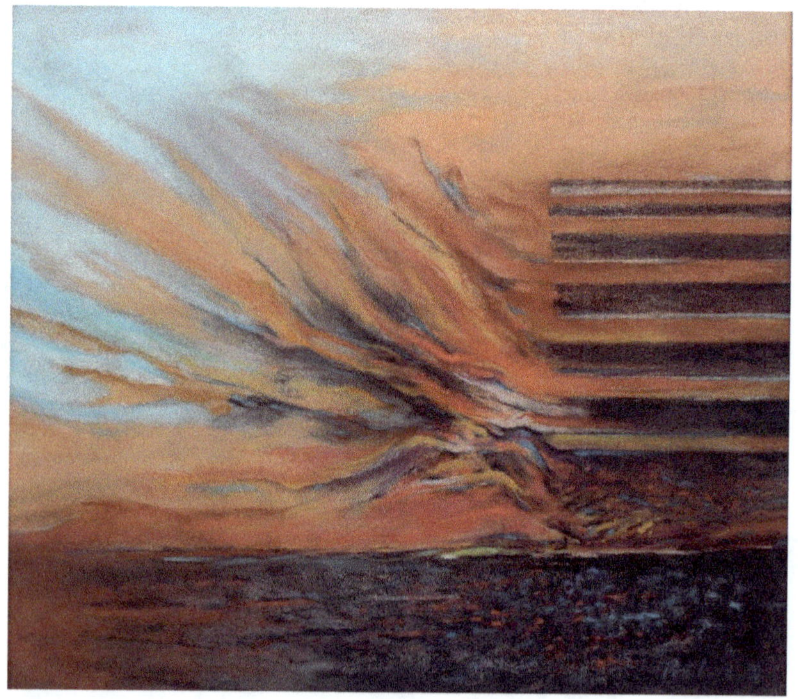

Swimming Inside the Fire

Least what they seem, most things are,
when you swim inside the fire.

Matchsticks lay down,
Flare with instrinsic blue passion
In sync with volcanic eruptions.

Neon ghosts gleam,
Dance in the glow and glare
Of the wildfire's beat.

Swimming inside the fire
On a white-hot orange peel,
Moons turn inside out.

Diamonding into blue sapphire
Stars reverse their spin.

A sultry rhythmic undulation
Mesmerizes,
Creeps in on satin panther paws.

Inside
Is out.

Outside
Is in.

Least what they seem, Most things are,
When you swim inside the fire.

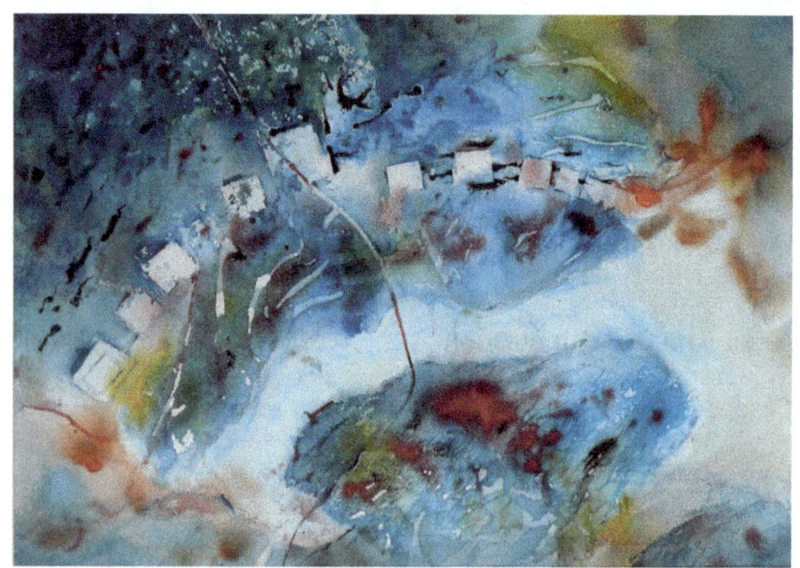

The Seventh Fountain of Yang

In the seventh Fountain of Yang
The heiroglyphs spin in metaphors
Along the coastal settlement
Twinning the edge of eternity.

Shadow, white and gold
A universal flame of knowledge
Reflecting a sapphire sky.

Standing in the separation
Of man's completed trilogy,
Mind, body and spirit
Melt through each other
In a surreal glowing heat.

Energy exponential,
Leaping in quantum footsteps,
Turns to liquid dreams
Tunneling through phasing moons
That roam the highway of stars.

In the seventh Fountain of Yang
Liquid light entities blaze and burn
Into a cinder of winds
And pearl vapors,
Scattering hieroglyphs
Into the eye of life's axis
Squaring the circle of death's paradigm.

The wheel of eternity spins.
Sparks fly beneath its thrust
Lighting the long-lost pathway
To the coastal settlement
And the seventh Fountain of Yang.

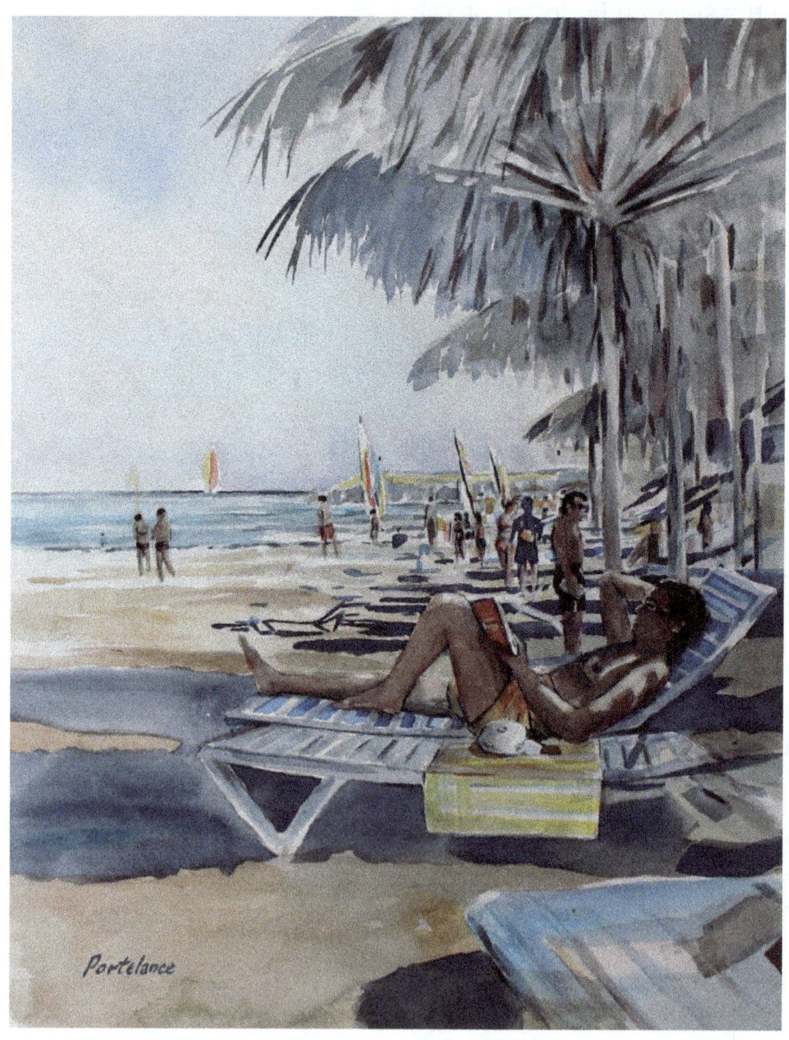

Portelance

The Reader

The reader escapes to the beach:
To get away from it all,
To enjoy the sun and sea,
To feel the sand between his toes,
To relax with nature,
To be suspended
Between earth and sky.

Boredom sets in.
The reader moves away
From the sun and sea
Into the shade of a tree;
Sits above the feel of the sand
On a wooden cot
And opens a book to escape.

The reader reads,
Mind travels to another country
Far from the sun and sea
Where a dank fog creeps through
A dark star-stripped evening,
On a desolate street
Of shadowy figures.

A chilled breeze
Invades the beach, the book and the reader.
The sun hints at setting.

The reader closes the book
And escapes
Back to reality.

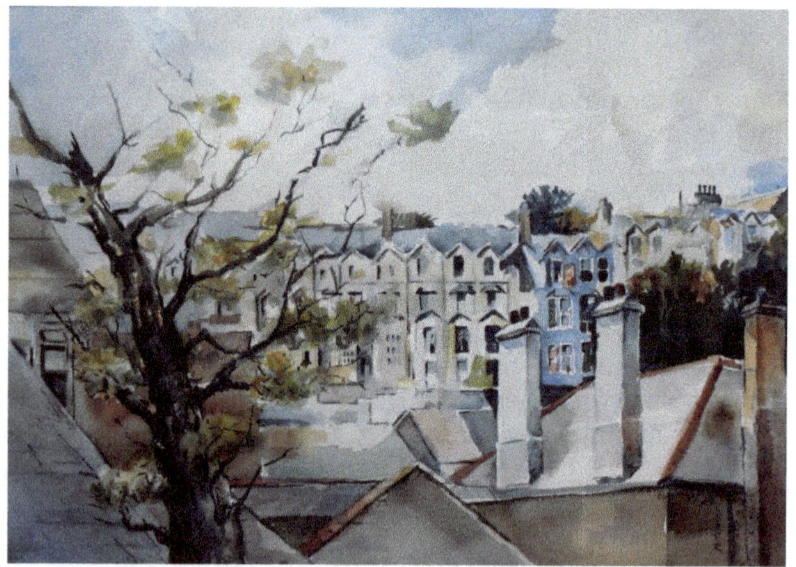

Surreal Townscape

Over a surreal townscape
Crowded with emptiness,
Dawn breaks
While the city still sleeps.
Empty streets and windows
Bear witness to the silence of the dogs,
The absence of the people,
The whisper of the wind.

Faint echoes and remnants
Of the fallen evening past
Still lay on the doorsteps,
They evaporate noiselessly
With the coming of the sun, T
he yellowing of the sky.

Somewhere,
Behind one of these windows,
In a crumbling crevice of tears,
A heart is pounding, pulsating
Within its fractured cracks.

Dawn oozes like liquid diamonds,
Shimmers and slides
Under the doorways,
Climbs the stairs
Toward the sound of the pounding heart,
Searching for a remnant of hope
Within its fractured cracks.

Dawn breaks,
Like a cracked heart
Over a jagged, surreal townscape
And bleeds through the empty streets.

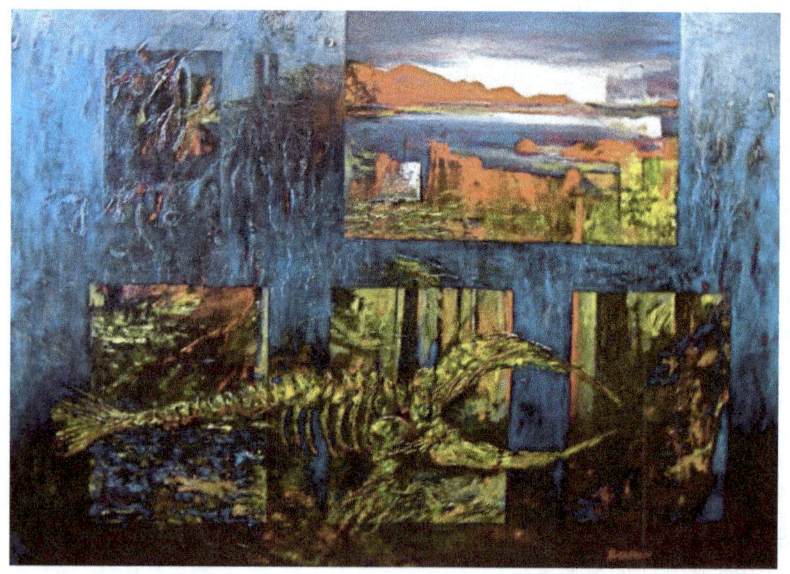

Whale Song

A haunting sound
Windows through the reeds,
Crawls on the soft sandy floor of the deep;
Rope, claw and a blue world swaying
Beneath red mounds of ant hill people,
Scurry through blue days
And a blur of restless nights.

Beneath our daily living
The whales languish
In waves of tranquil whispers.
Singing in sacred frequencies,
Caressing the underbelly of the living ocean,
They compose focused symphonies.

These water bound mammals,
Our alien brothers and sisters of sorts,
Have learned the secret
Of living in peace and harmony:
No underwater nuclear wars;
No oil refineries;
No tar sands;
No power hungry residents
In the aquatic world.

The whales,
The most powerful denizens of the deep,
The unchallenged rulers of the sea
Swim with the sharks
They usually don't destroy them.

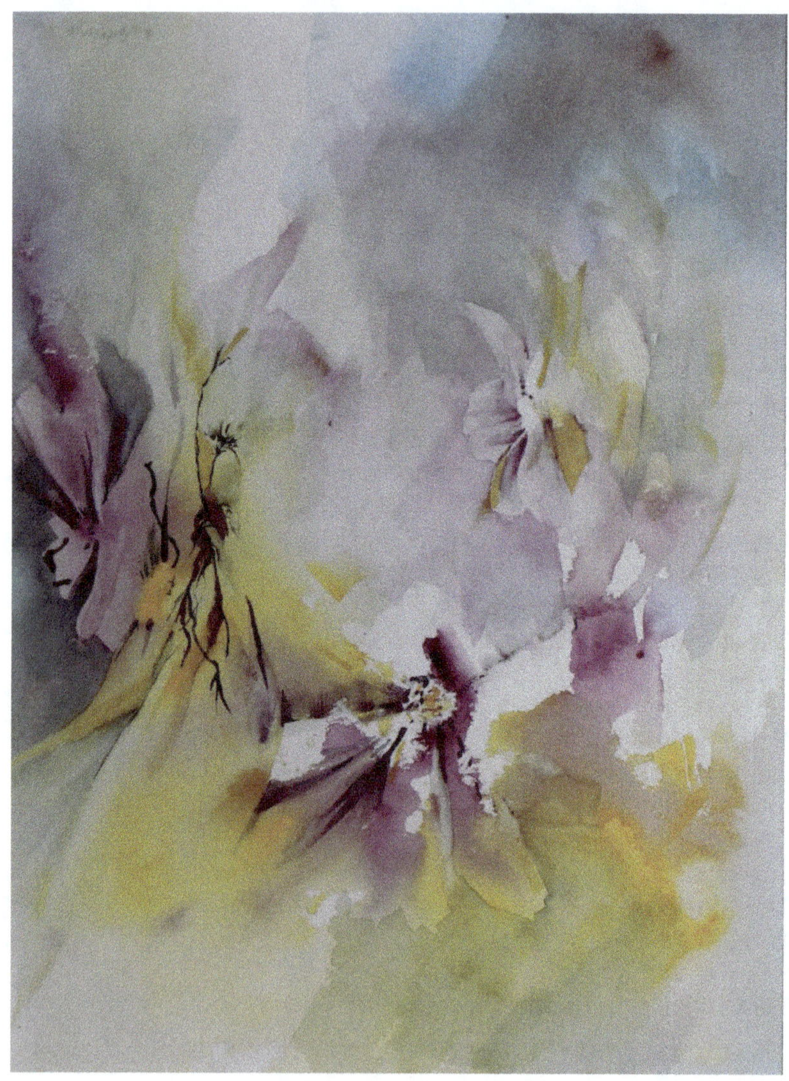

Falling Through Infinity

Falling through infinity,
Gracing the tunnels of time,
They whirl and swirl
In a windswept world of their own.

Fairy dust, Pixie wings
Glazing through gold and lavender puzzles,
Nuzzling the edge of colour
In an opal and topaz dream.

On the creamy underside of a blue note
The lilac shades of melody
Linger and waltz with memories,
Encapsulated in this wonderland
Ruled by fantasy's fancy.

There are dancers, jesters and queens
Courting the magical mood,
Cajoling the jolly king
To sing another chorus
Of "a pocketful of rye".

Sliding through suspended chords
And jazz master moves,
The fairies fly away,
Falling through infinity
To lay in the lap of plenty,
To sleep...
Perchance to dream.

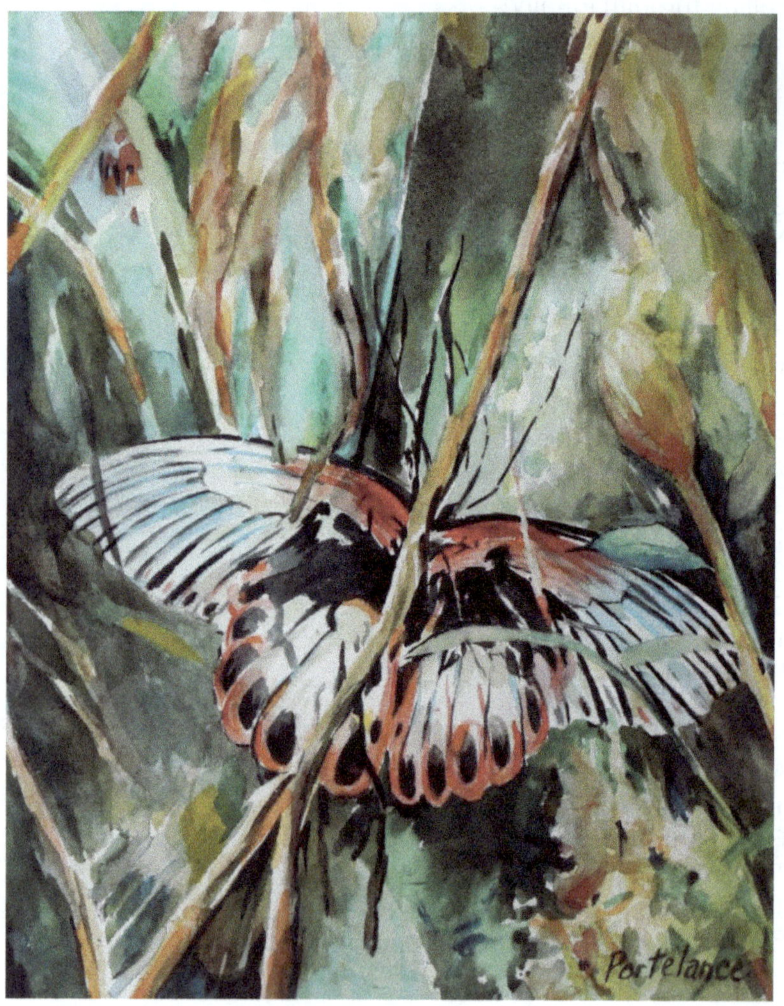

Winged Masquerade

She sings atop a waterfall
Into a hollow log
Rafting the tides of time
Under a crimson sky of changing moods.

On the other side of the stick
They dance at the masquerade ball
On a liquid floor of waves,
Under an overlapping crimson sky of changes.

The story is there for all to see,
The story of the wings:
Chapter seven
Page six
Paragraph three,
Cinderella wishing her life away,
Waiting for her prince,
Slipper in hand,
To mount his steed,
And cross the winged bridge
To make her dreams come true.

She sings atop a waterfall.
In the distance he hears her voice.
She hears his steed's hooves
The time for dreams is at hand.

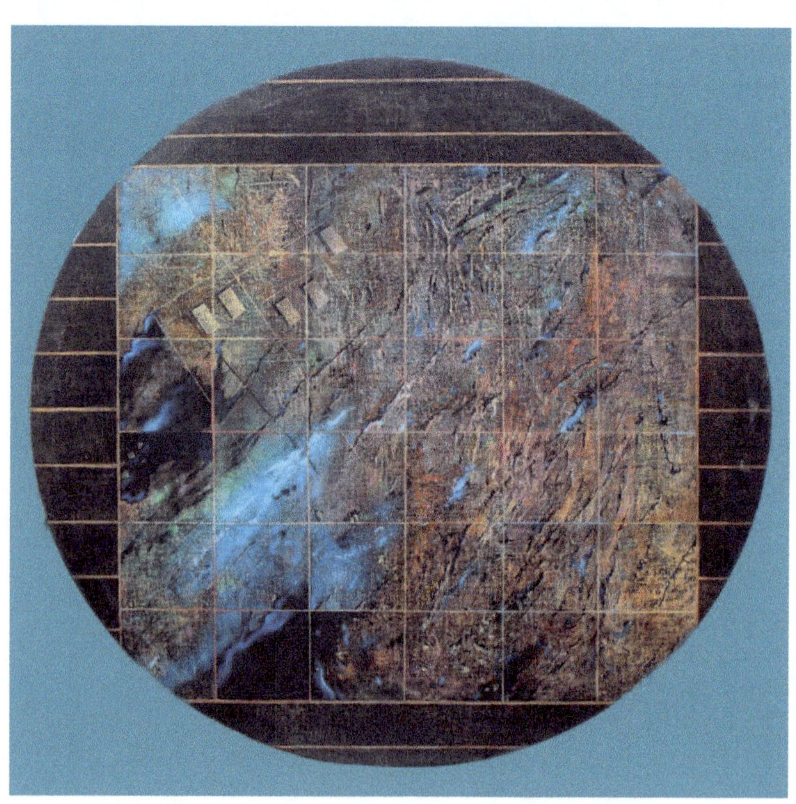

Circle Squared

A square in a circle in a square,
Windows in a world within a world;
The shadows of ghost sharks
Pummel up river through stone and sand
Uprooting Van Goghs and Monets,
Searching for Turners and Cezannes,
Carving their breath into the atmosphere,
Staining the Canvas with life,
Become a masterpiece
In a square in a circle in a square.

The windows have invisible eyes and mouths.
They shed tears and grow smiles,
Chameleon themselves to fit
The mood of the painting;
To ride the ghost sharks;
To turn the stone and sand
Into diamonds of great worth.

Trading in secrets and mysteries,
Magnetized by haunting chants
And trapped in strange madrigals,
The windows have grown weary
Of their world within a world
And shattered into an illusion.
Uprooted trees are disintegrating
The ghost sharks are shape shifting
Into a new species.

A new reality is surfacing.
A circle in a square in a circle,
Wet, slick, damp, inviting...
Water world!

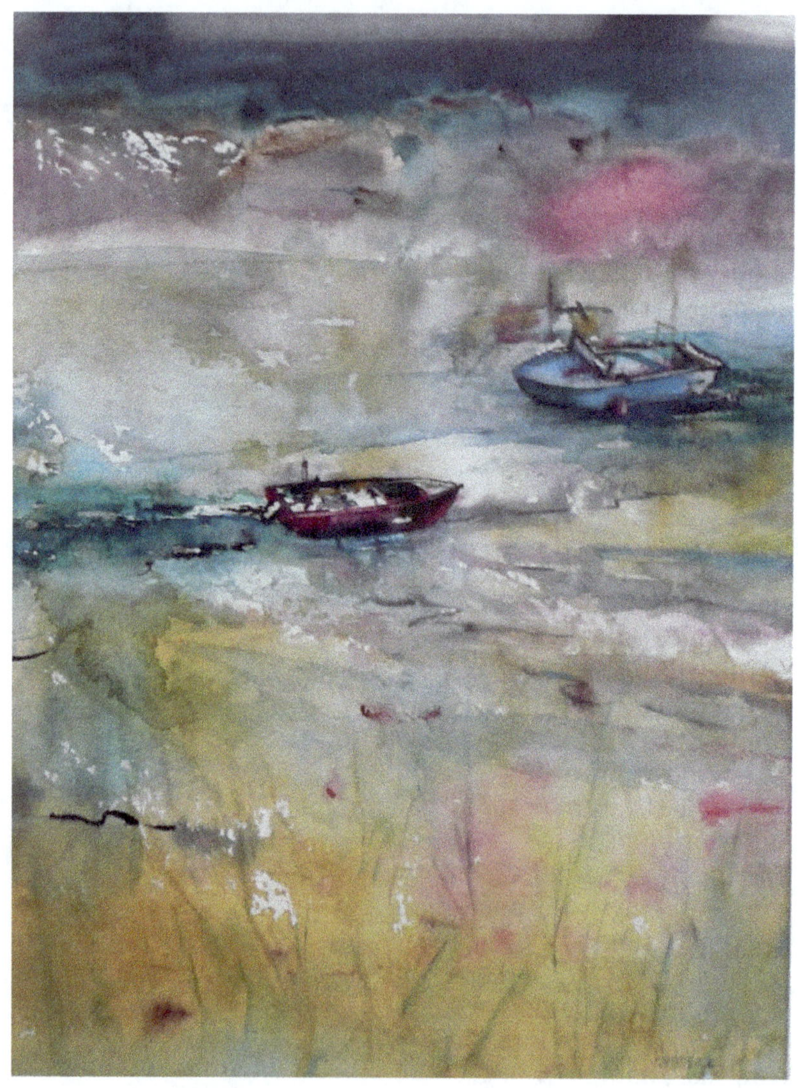

Tidal Flats

I rise in golds and yellows
In the pink reflection of a sunrise
And walk the tidal flats of my mind.

Glorious muted, blue tones
Shackle my wrists,
Draw me into their music.
I sway like a lonely leaf
Making love to the breeze.

I move into a white grooved moment
Then sail on a purple ship of dreams
Into uncharted territory
Exploring my psyche inside out.

I drift away toward a blue skiff,
Board it with wet feet
And fiery eyes,
Anticipating the next horizon.
So light this balsa boat.
So airy this feeling of enchantment.

I float upward to a surreal coastal town,
Hanging below the mist line,
At the base of a mountain calling my name.
The high snows know me.
I am no stranger to the cold.

I climb into the pink hole in the sky.
I pulsate and dimensionalize
Onto the tidal flats
Of someone else's dream.

I rise in golds and yellows
And make their dream my own.

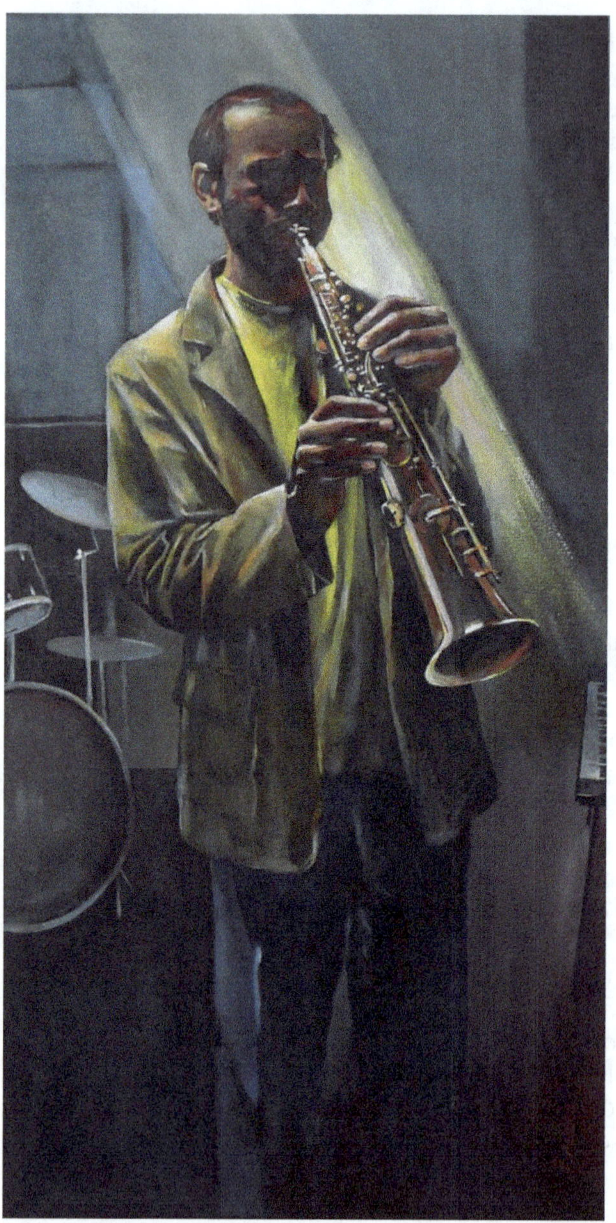

Sweet, Honeyed Dewdrops

Sweet like honeyed dewdrops,
The notes flutter and fly
Through the room like little sparrows
Loosed from his gentle feathered touch.
He kisses the reed with a tender torment
That spills through the mute atmosphere
Like a split nickel right on the money.

The horn moves and speaks.
The frequency peaks.
His fingers turn to sharp silver hammers
Pounding excitement into the crowd
In a fury of fevered need.

The music rebels and bleeds through his horn
Until it's a rhapsody torn and reborn
Into a platinum cradled sigh.
Swinging and swaying
A feeling is playing
His soliloquy of the human condition.

A fever in the soul,
A lump in the throat,
A symphony loosed from his horn,
It's a beautiful noise
That tugs at the heart
And turns the moon inside out.

Weary fingers snub the rhythm
The song slowly fades away;
But the taste of the sweet, honeyed dewdrops
Still lingers on the mind's palate.

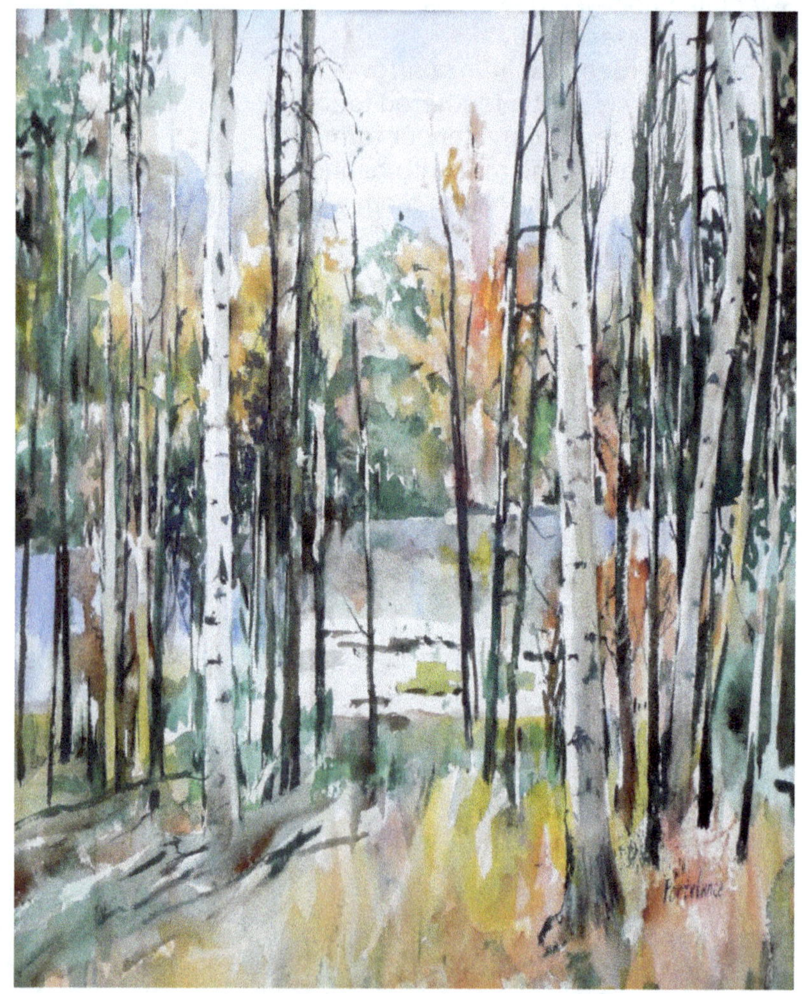

The Tree Whisperer

Mellowed past the point of fascination,
Swaying in a world of exultation,
Leaves fall from trees like crepe paper and wool.
In the afterglow of Nature's pull
Reflections peek through this gentle shine
On water repast turned to splendid wine.
As sparkling Chardonnay flows through the mind,
Lights spools and pools then starts to unwind.

And all the while the tree whisperer listens.
And all the while the silent lake glistens.

Perchance there be an eagle flying by.
Perhaps a teardrop falling from his eye
As autumn leaves in full state of undress
Lay patient, waiting for fall to confess
That she's fallen prey to winter's charms
And seeks comfort in his icy arms.

And all the while the tree whisperer listens.
And all the while the silent lake glistens.

I watch not sands in the hourglass.
Nor care I for hours as they pass.
I lay here with ear pressed to the ground
In silence listening for the sound
Of footsteps foretelling your return.
In icy flames of sorrow I burn.

And all the while the tree whisperer listens.
And all the while the silent lake glistens.

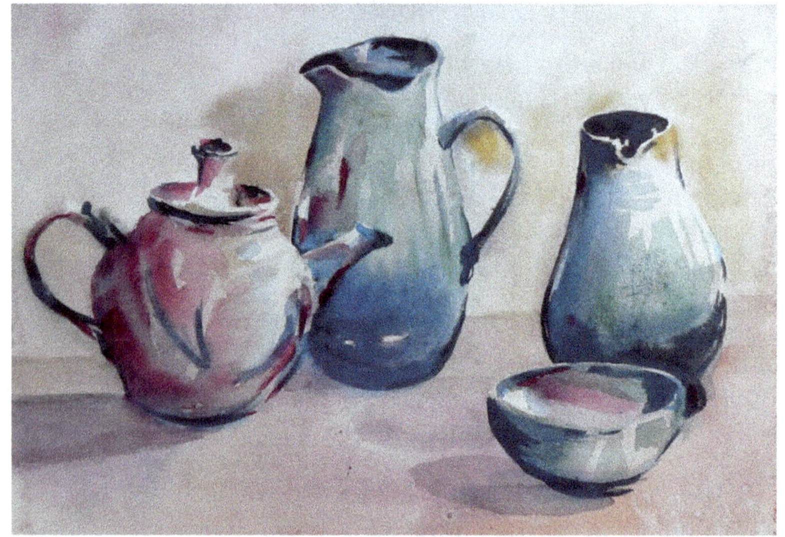

Crumbled To Dust

Hands, now icy cold,
Crumbled to dust,
Once coursing with blood, warmth
And the fire of creativity.

Did this gifted artisan laugh too loudly?
Love too deeply?
Did he don masks to hide his tears
And wear paper smiles in public?
Did he weep openly
And parade his scars for all to see
On a stage of his own making?
Was the stage solid?
Or did he build it on weak and shifting sand.
Did he give one too many performances?
Or did he leave them aching for an encore.

As he gasped his final breath
Did his hands feign applause
As they lay limply on his chest?
Or did he feebly try to wring them in angst.

Registration number 91750 et. al.
These pieces of fine Coal Port China
Remain locked in life's prison.
The hands that crafted them have escaped
With the angel of death.

I remain incarcerated,
Eyes fixed on these ornaments,
Very much aware of my own hands
Soon to be icy cold,
Crumbled to dust.

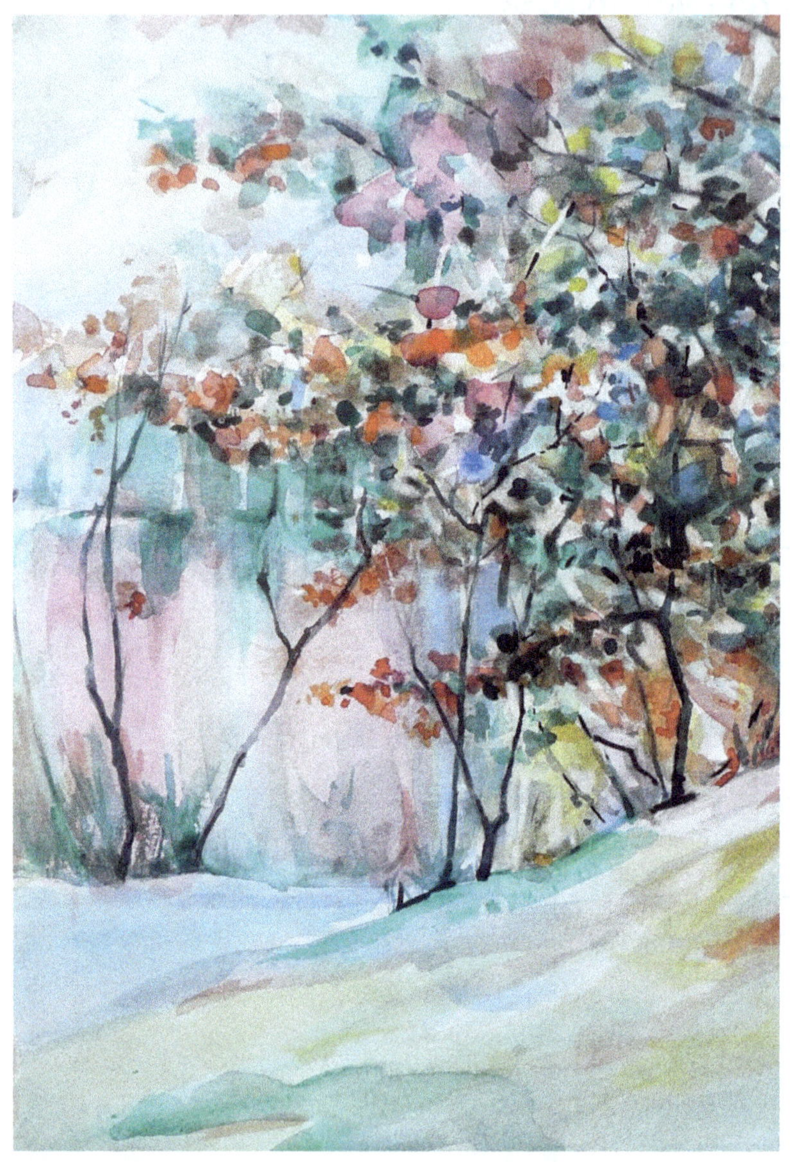

Autumn's Approach

A world spinning. Seasons changing.
Technicolour wizardry on display.

Autumn approaches In high heel sneakers,
Padding in surreptitiously:
A blur of green, yellow, gold, red;
A splash of purple, lilac, pink blue;
Streaking on strands of dew covered grass,
Dancing in fields of dreams well spent.
Under a burnished sky,
The summer sun is turning to dust,
Disappearing.

A world spinning,
Seasons changing,
Slipping and sliding
On raindrops,
Bumping and grinding against the breeze,
In nature's surreal and sultry strip tease
As summer burns out,
Trips,
Falls,
Into autumn's waiting embrace.

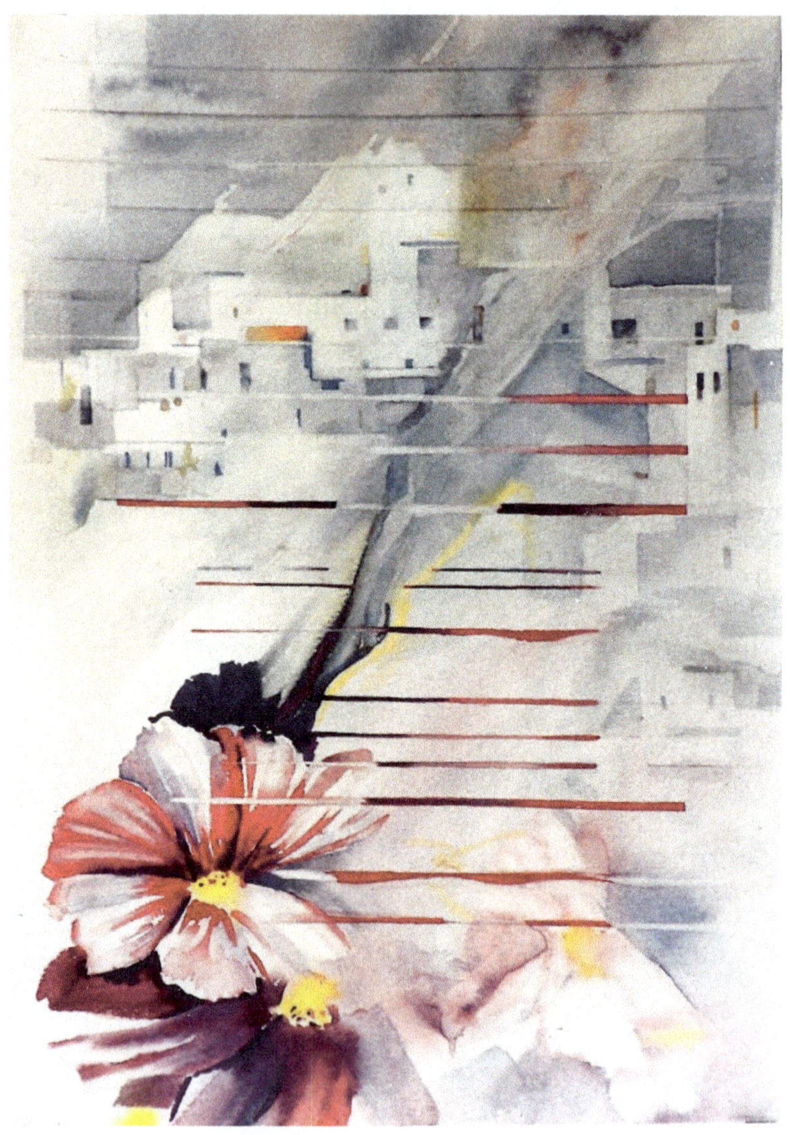

A Flower for Helen

On the rising knowledge of colour and tone
The steps are stacked like books.
A phantom man stands
A flower clasped in his thoughts...
A flower for Helen.

The beauty and softness of the petals
Cling to the air
Like her scent on his collar.

He climbs the steps with expectation,
With the flower he hopes will please her.
He moves as mist,
Higher and higher,
Toward the gates of heaven.

As he nears, he hears
A stir of wings and whispers.
Slowly the whispers dissipate
Until there is only one voice.

Indistinct at first,
Slowly growing louder,
He hears her calling his name.

As she approaches him,
He kisses the flower,
Places it in her outstretched hand.

A flower for Helen
At journey's end,

They rest
In a peaceful, easy feeling. It is enough.

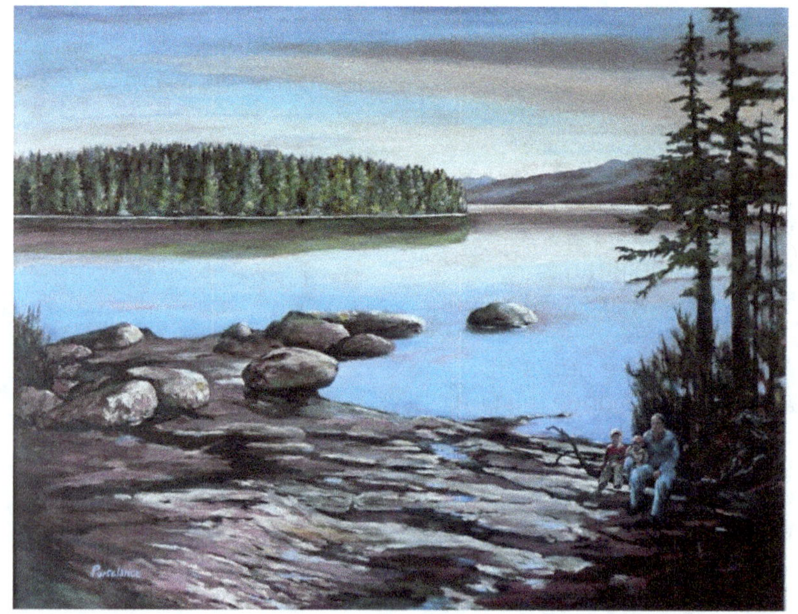

At the Cabin

We're a closer knit
In the womb of time
In this midst of nature's
Green and blue enchantment
That surrounds us,
Infuses the atmosphere
With beauty and love.

Slick, like the rocks,
We slip and slide
Through our hearts
And rest in the lap
Of a quiet passion.

We are one.
Woven tightly together
With understanding,
We give birth to a serenity
That is ours alone.

We are the trees,
The water,
The rocks,
The sky.

I am you. You are me. We are one

We're a closer knit
At the cabin.

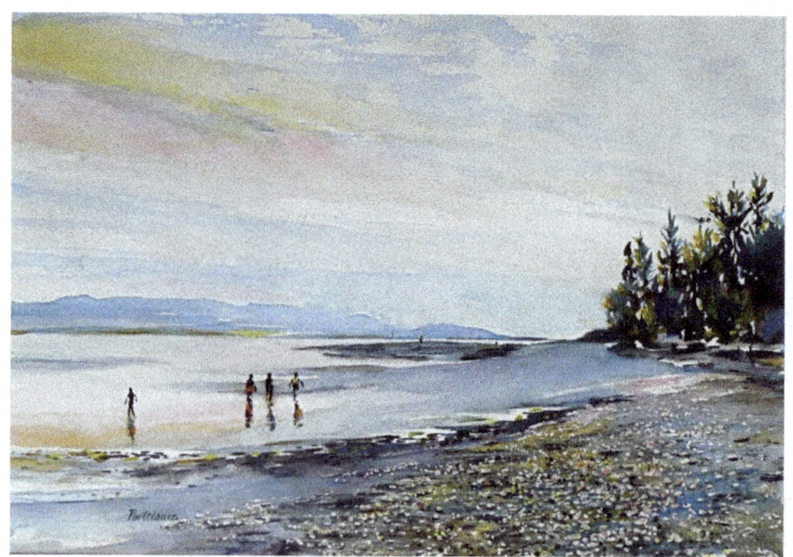

The Pastels

They glide on the pastels
In the bright shadow of a passing moment,
Beachcombers warmed by the cool of the water,
As the wind rubs back and forth
Polishing them to a perfect shine.

There is a glistening,
A gleaming inside this passing moment,
That lingers and rests on their shoulders.

The invisible sun smolders
Behind a slow moving cloud,
Primping and preening
For its entrance
Into the pastels.

Like a seasoned alchemist,
The sun flexes its fingers
And transforms the pastels
Into a golden dream.

Later,
Gliding on their shadows,
The beachcombers sew the sun
Into a twilight robe
And lay it on the pastels.

As the darkness undresses,
Gliding on their fading shadows,
The beachcombers fade away.

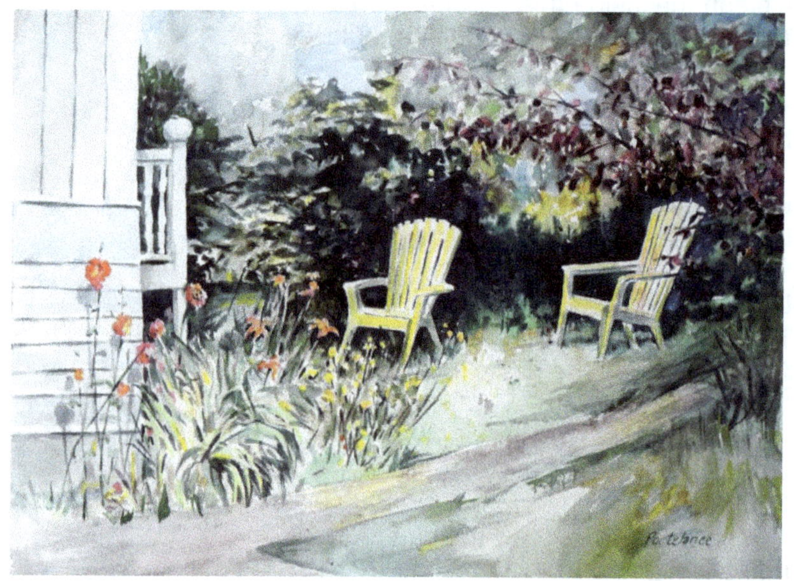

The Yellow Chairs

They sit there whispering,
The pale ghosts,
Relaxing
In the yellow chairs.

Sometimes they manifest
As a formless mist,
Shifting position,
In the yellow chairs.

In their minds
The flowers haven't changed.
The grass is still freshly cut.
The house remains the same,
As do they,
Inside their eternal now.

They pass each afternoon together
Commenting on the flowers,
Discussing the weather,
Quite amazed
At how time passes
When it doesn't...

When they're relaxing
In the yellow chairs.

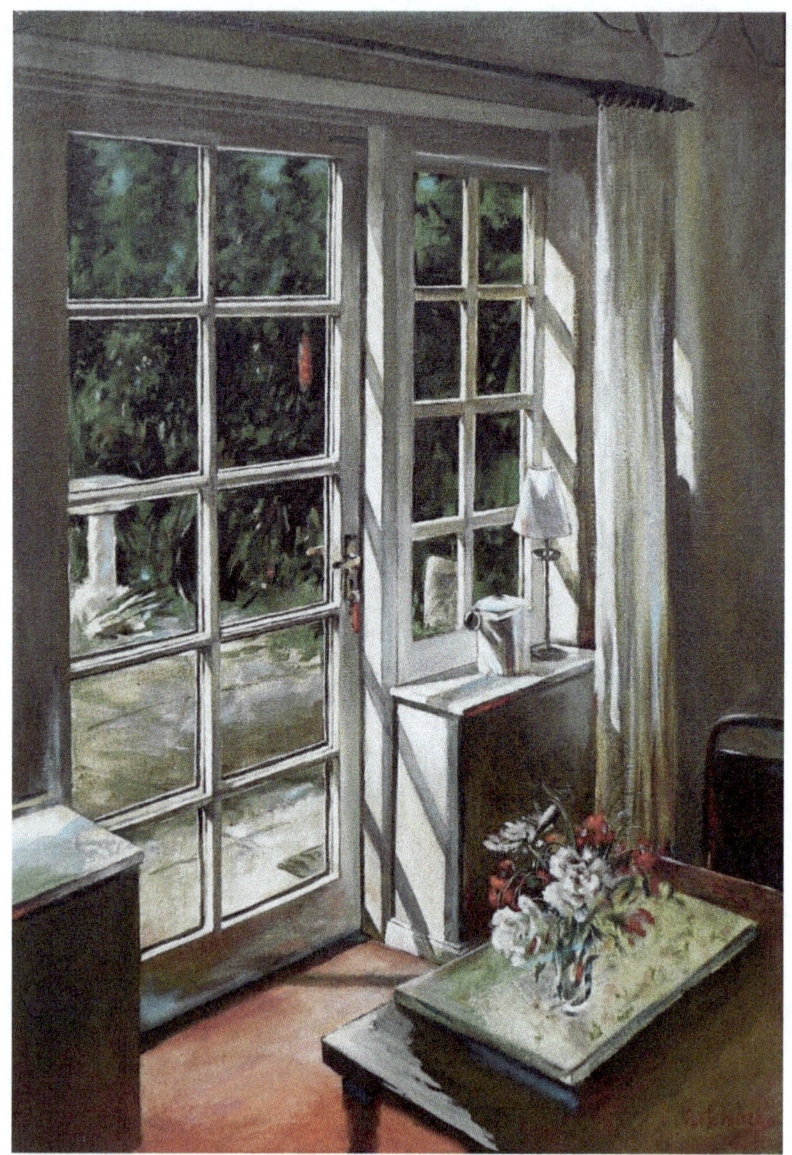

Outside, Inside

Twenty windows in the French doors;
Eyes to the outside, inside;
A picture within. A painting without
Blended in layers of atmospheric beauty.

How many migrating birds
Have rested on the gleaming white pedestal,
Stark against the crushed velvet tree-scape
Back-dropping nature's easel?

The windows whisper to each other:
Recalling the sparrows,
Remembering the crows
And smiling now
At the furry black squirrel
That scampers across the patio
Onto the lawn,
Skittering up the ivory pedestal base
Then disappearing
Into the green velvet world and home.

Dusk approaches.
The long shadows encroach.
The whispers of the windows wane,
Blending into a composite dream,
As evening soars in
On a flurry of raven wings.

Night unfolds her arms, embraces the scene.
A veil of summer rain begins to shawl
And lingers like a French kiss.
The lights dim outside.

Inside, the French doors
And the world fall asleep.

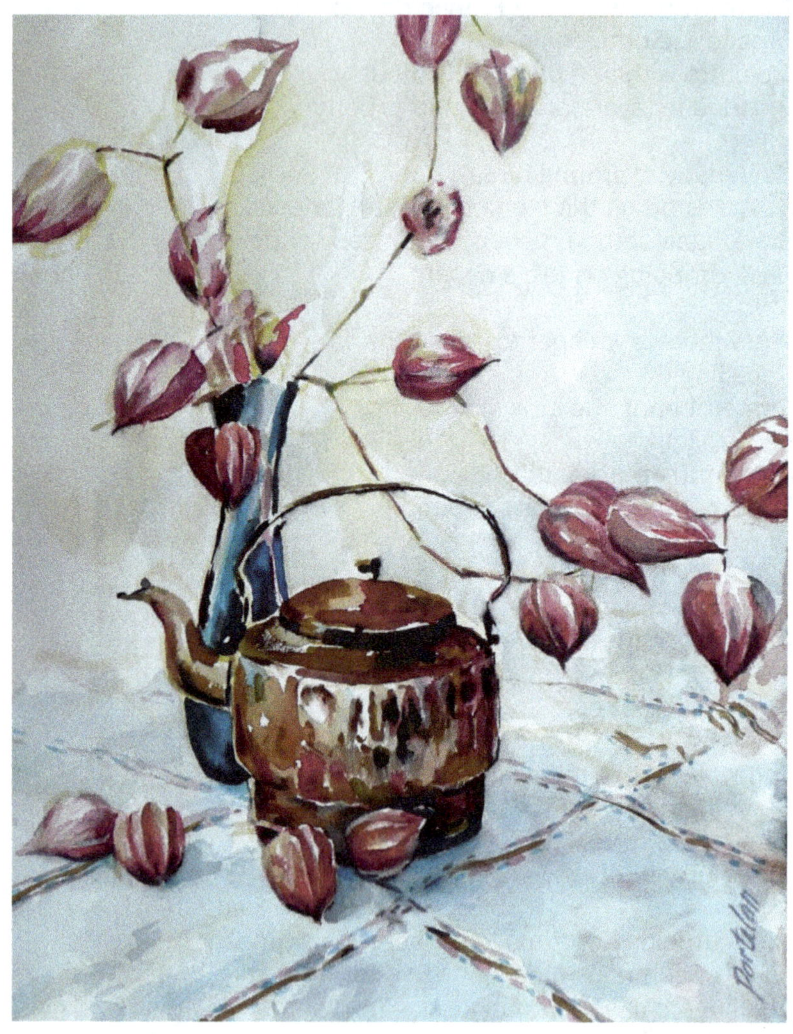

Teapot Strangers

Outside a porcelain ring
They mill and dance,
Embrace and prance,
On the midriff of the copper teapot;
Strangers in contemporary dress,
Mixing and mingling
On its merry-go-round periphery.

In the glisten and shine
Of Aztec and wine
A neo-jazz melody plays
In bold supersonic waves.
Flowers of time
Sway and unwind
In a frenzy of silent drum beats.
Divining down
Like bruised ivy vine rods
Searching for cool water piano keys
To soothe the fevered air.

The flowers dive and fall
At the feet of the teapot strangers,
Seemingly un-noticed,
Unrequired;
But something surreal is happening here.
The teapot strangers have stopped dancing.
A stillness pervades.
An invisible fragrance invades.

The flowers and teapot strangers
Have transcended the dimensional divide.

As their two worlds collide
A porcelain ring dissolves.

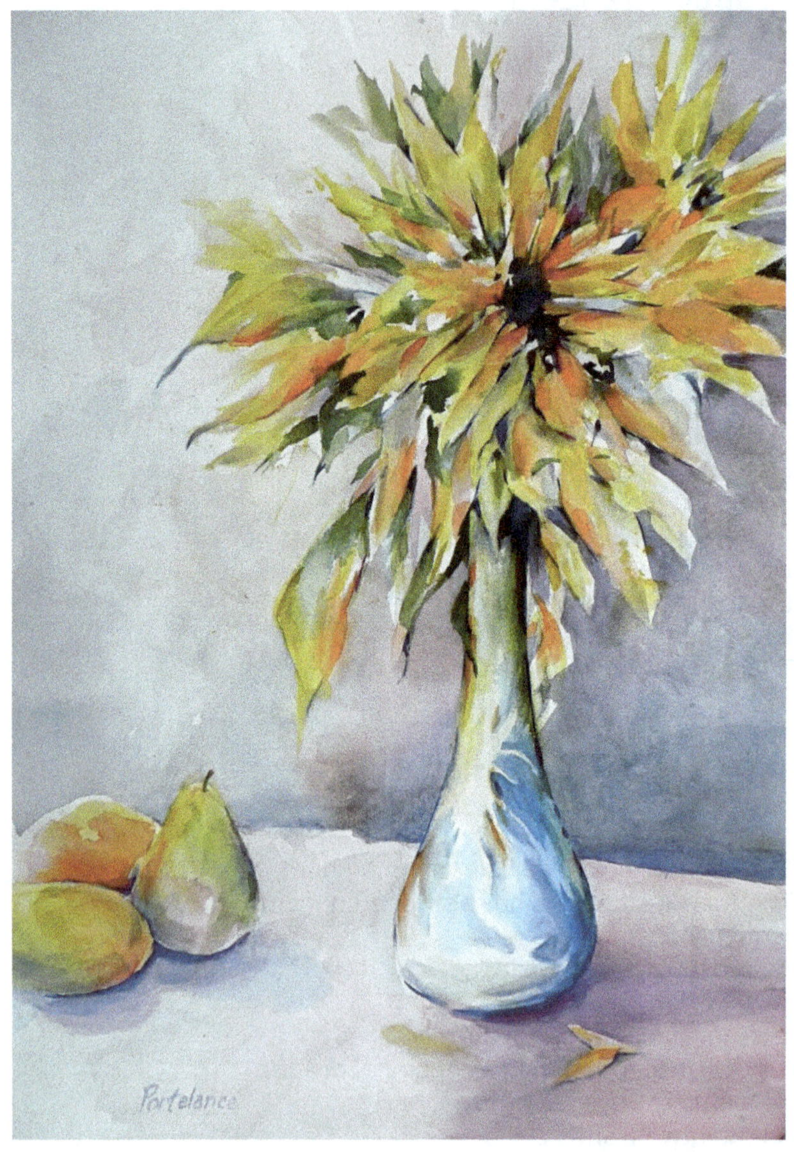

Flower Fantasy Land

Through the dark doorway,
In the centre of the mild, orange excitement,
Voices whisper and beckon
In sugar sweet overtones
And perfumed visions.
Liquid secrets seep
From burnished amber, nectar pods
Hidden deep inside caverns
Lurking behind the dark doorway.

On the surface
The flowers rustle with comments.
The fruit on the table listens intently
To the story of the flowers
Unfolding in windblown chapters
From the diaries of the petals.

It's five o'clock somewhere
In a rush hour world
All the time;
But in this corner of the room,
In this slice of insanity
At the edge of a broken universe,
It's just another lazy, routine day
Filled with mild, orange excitement
In flower fantasy land.

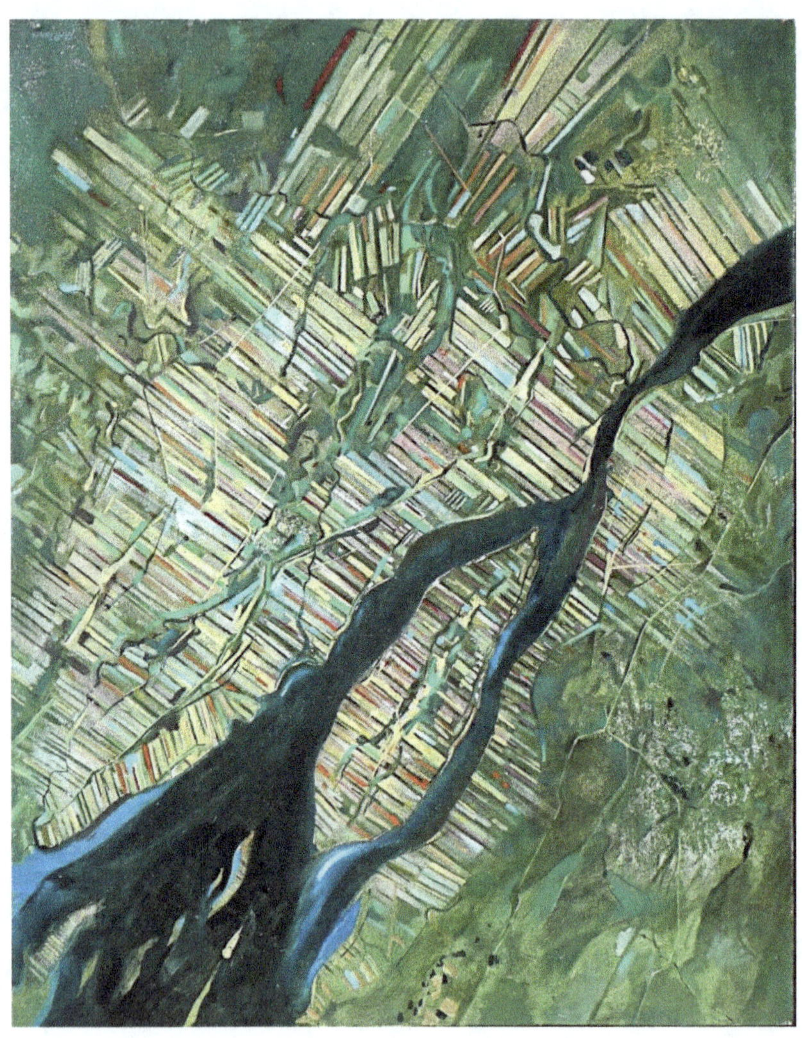

Twenty-Six Forty-Four

Indistinction abounds:
The result of mind invasions
And body abrasions;
Metal melted to glass,
Bland and foggy,
To be less distinct.

The copper faced alien intruder,
Body of ebony and lapis,
Welded to the blinds,
Sits drawing refracted light,
Weaving it into patterns
To enhance the earthling tree figure
That flows across the floor
In liquid movements
Of dolomite and diamond,

This is the future.
We become least what we are
In a silicon dream of neon vines,
Indistinct, non-descript entities,
The face of inevitable change...
An extinction of sorts
In a broken glass menagerie
Of things inhuman
In the year 2644.

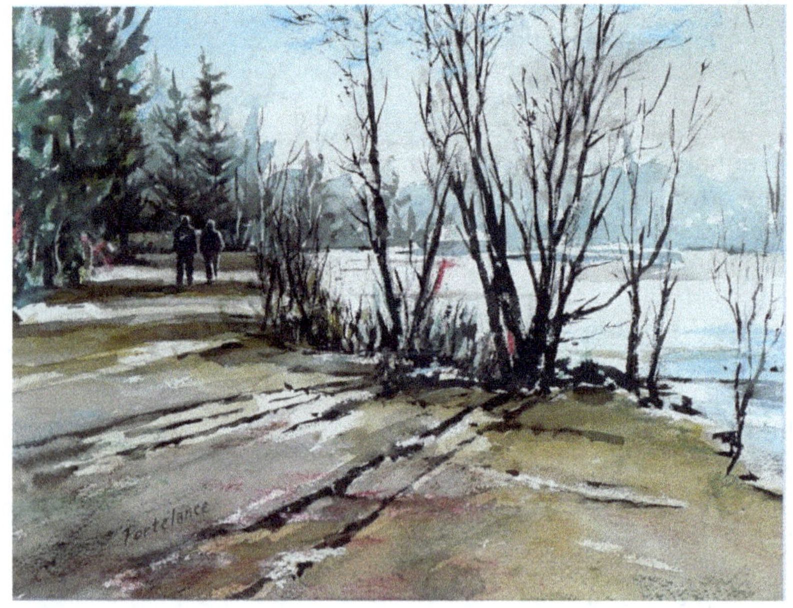

Shadow and Light

In shadow and light
They walk through eternity
On the day that never was,
But always is.

They time travel
Through their own dreams
Never together,
But never apart.

They are the perfect anachronism
Unto themselves and eternity;
Shadows revolving in the light,
Light spinning inside the shadows.
Always beginning,
Forever changing,
Never ending,
They are the ripples
On the waters of the sky;
The thunder and lightning
Beneath the raging sea;
The placid lake, the rolling river.

Time spirals through itself,
Weaves through the other side of its coil
Worm-holing through the fabric of dreams,
Crocheting them into origami movies,
Black and white film noirs.

In shadow and light
They walk through eternity
Never together,
But never apart,
On a day that never was,
But always is.

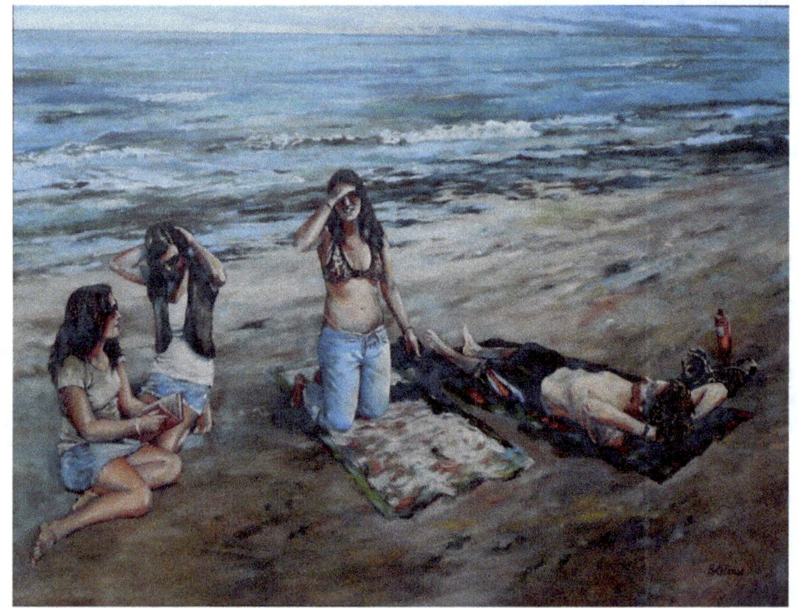

Canadians on Juno Beach

The reader,
The hairdresser,
The sentinel
And the sleeper;
All together
On the beach of another country...
In another time and space in their thoughts.

Canadians on Juno Beach:
Touching the sand,
Smelling the sea,
Gazing at eternity's horizon.

The day rolls by:
To the beat of the incoming waves,
To the beat of their hearts,
To the feint whispers
Of eagle wings beating
And pale ghosts drifting
Somewhere out of sight
Beyond the patchwork horizon.

The novel,
The brush,
The salute,
And the repose.

The Canadians on Juno Beach,
The beach of another country...
In another time and space in their thoughts.

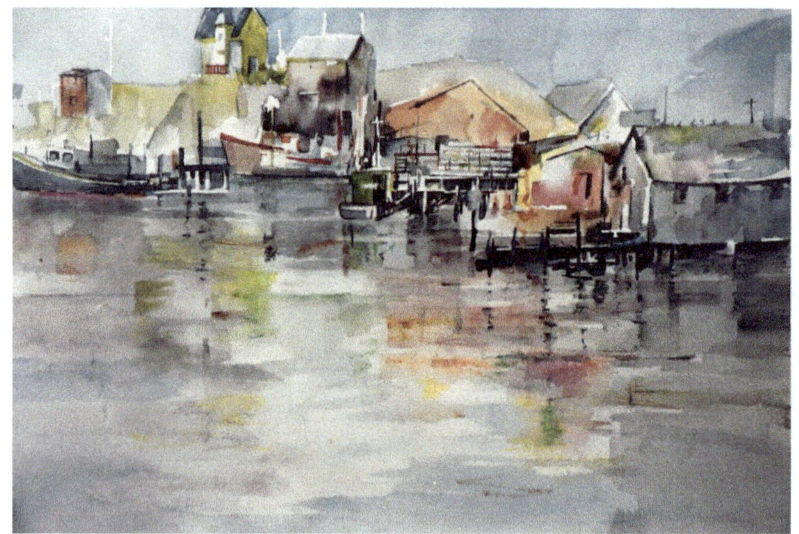

Antique Harbour

The gold drift of sea shine
Speckled with shimmering pastels
Reflections of a landscape on the wing
        Dips, brush like,
Into the chameleon waters of the bay.

A stained glass antique harbour
Of broken shiplap and dulled hardwood,
Peeling paint and barnacled hulls
Decorates the boats that have fallen ill
In the jaws of disrepair.

This is the way of the old men and the sea.
Lacklustre fishermen.
Past their prime,
Past the point of no return,
Living out their salty days
On the tears of an ebbing tide.

Once there were tall ships,
Gleaming fishing vessels,
Muscular young men
With a fever in their soul
And their heart set like a sail.

Once there were younger days,
    Glistening boats,
    Gleaming hulls,
And too many fish to catch.

  Once upon a time,
    Long ago,
This harbour was alive.

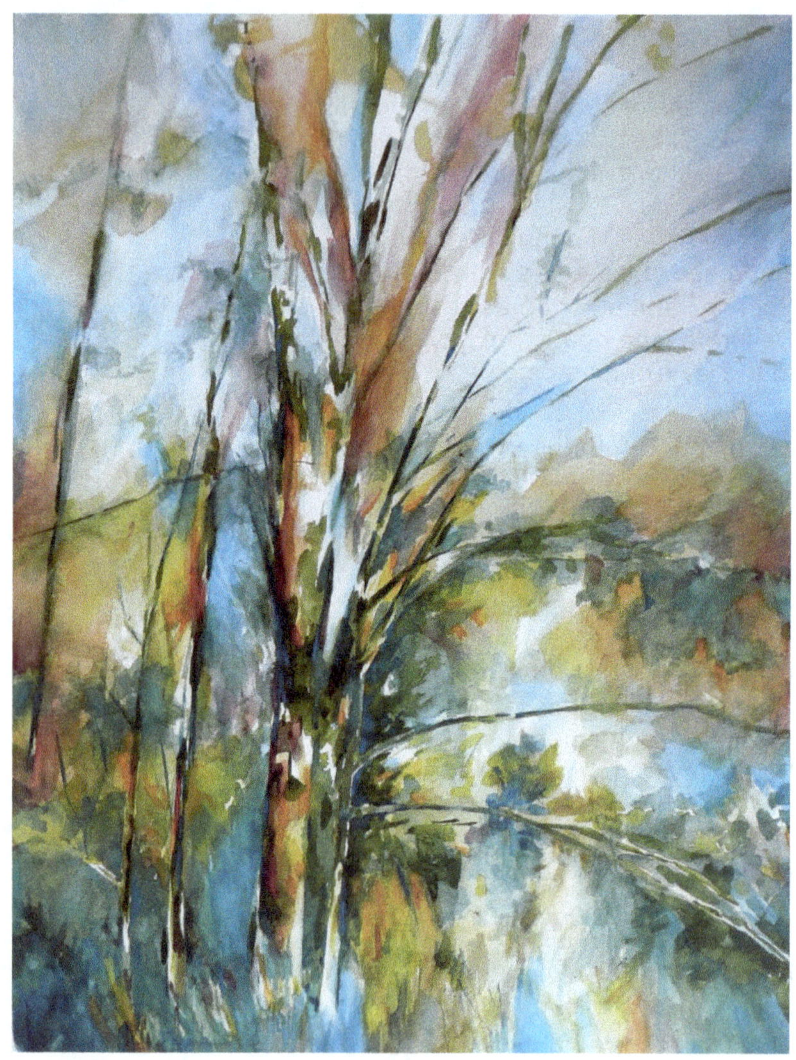

Signature

Full bodied, leafy trees,
Ink blots, smears of green,
Wisping and decorating,
The sky's blue blouse.

Unframed portraits of moving still life.
Smoky dreams dreaming
In a low lying, fog-encrusted horizon
Ushering in an early dusk.

        I sit,
Someplace between my signature
     And a half-written page.

I watch the world
In slow motion fade out,
Waiting for the darkness to edge in.

I watch the waning light
Flow into the hard-edged corner
Of a burnt out star
And sign my name
To another day...
Passed away.

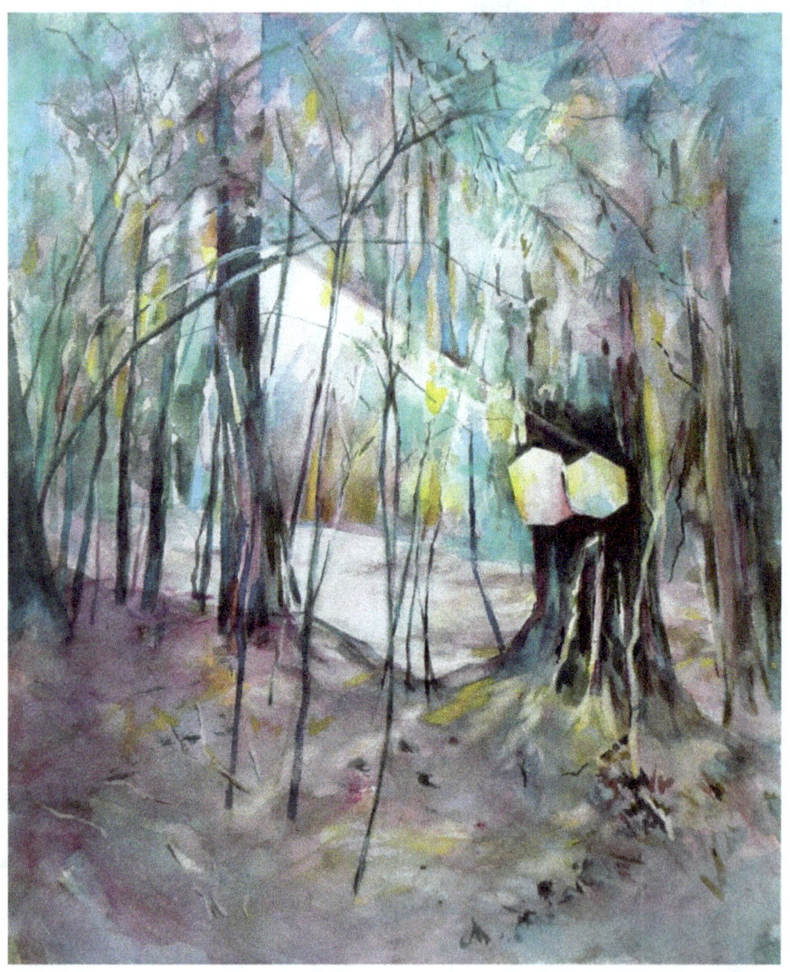

Summer Dream

Silk footsteps sink softly
In surreal indentations,
Carving indelible pathways
Into the disappearing shine
Of a marauding sun.
The wind whispers crimson secrets
Into the wrinkled face of the river.

In the eye of a summer dream
Trees stand in juried solitude
Contemplating an opaque sky of swirls.
Shadows of life scatter in between
Patches of bright and dark
Spreading what dreams may come
In salt and pepper patterns
Over the spotted landscape.

The easel in my mind
Resurrects itself
Into a pastel mood painting.
Leaves glide and slide,
Flip and flop
At the whim of the breeze.
In a chaotic, random flash dance.

    The lemon sun darkens,
        Turns to red
Then melts into a surreal pink gloss;
A half scoop of strawberry ice-cream
Swallowed up by the hungry horizon
    Dining at twilight's table
At the edge of a summer dream.

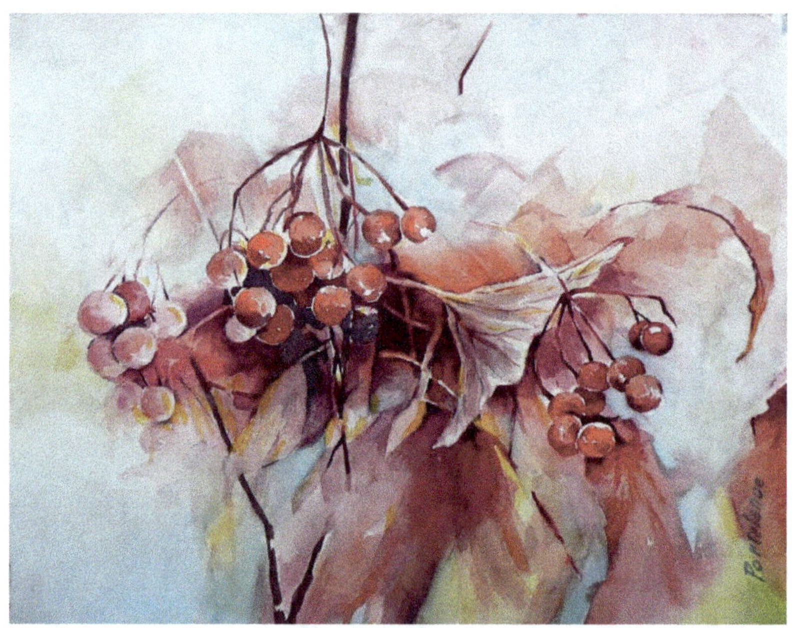

Splash of Red

Splash of red
Yells against muted tones of blue
Fire and ice,
Cold and hot,
Reminiscent of Candy apples,
Strawberry shortcake,
Raspberry ripple ice-cream.

A sting ray
On a pristine racetrack,
Carburetion of the soul
Gears up the eye's appetite
To feast on the splash
Of succulent red splendour.

The coveted cool of inspiration
Lights the soul on fire,
Whets the palette of life
And the muted tones of blue
Scream in a splash of red.

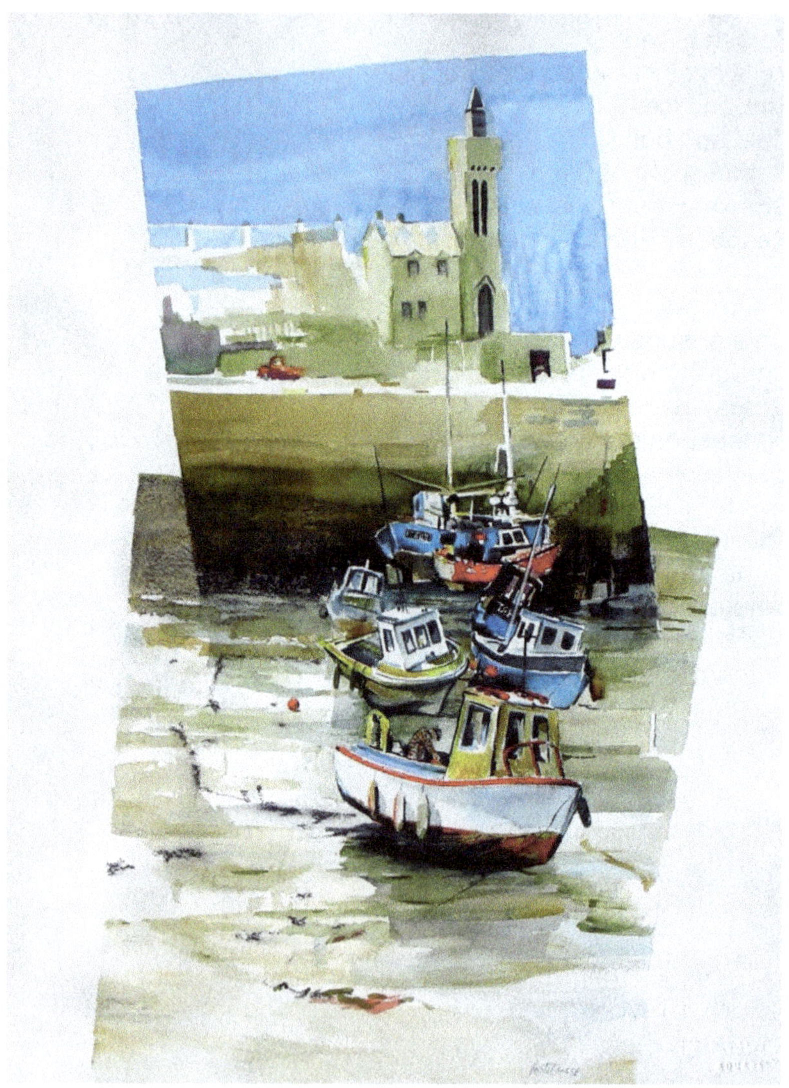

Yesterday's Harbour

Blocks of moving life
Stilled by the brush,
Spilled in a hush of paint
Onto a pale wine soaked day.

Drawn into the core of the mood,
The hungry eyes flit,
Excited birds on the wing,
Landing here,
Jumping there,
Backing up to push,
Like a taut violin bow
Drawn at break-neck speed
Over a slick sheet of tones.

A collage of super imposed mind postcards,
Drift at the edge of yesterday's harbour,
Enveloped in tears
Stamped with the tides of time,
Echoing a past
Lost in the present.

   The hungry eyes,
     Now sated,
       Droop.
      Lids close.

The harbour falls asleep.

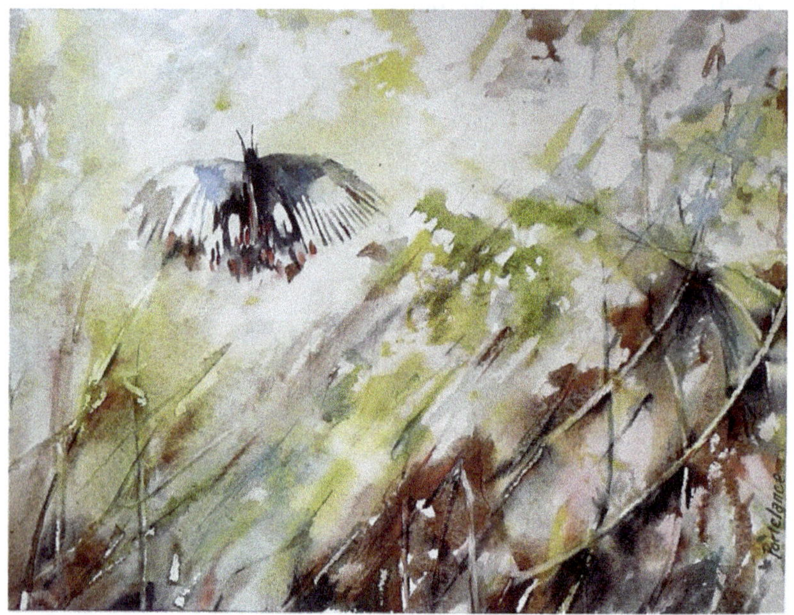

Butterfly Effect

Dark and light wafer wings flutter,
And beauty was born
For a moment like this:
Cleansed by a raindrop,
Towel dried by a zephyr
In a wonderland of pulsating colour.

Feather light,
Crepe paper wings,
Flying low
Through a world of blur.

Slow motion
Kaleidoscope lens
Zooms in on
Bright dancing with dark,
Magicians and angels
Playing with grasshoppers
In a vivid technicolour landscape.

    Blue and white,
    Shade and light,
    Nature's wizardry
      Creating
     The beauty,
     The dynasty,
    The butterfly effect.

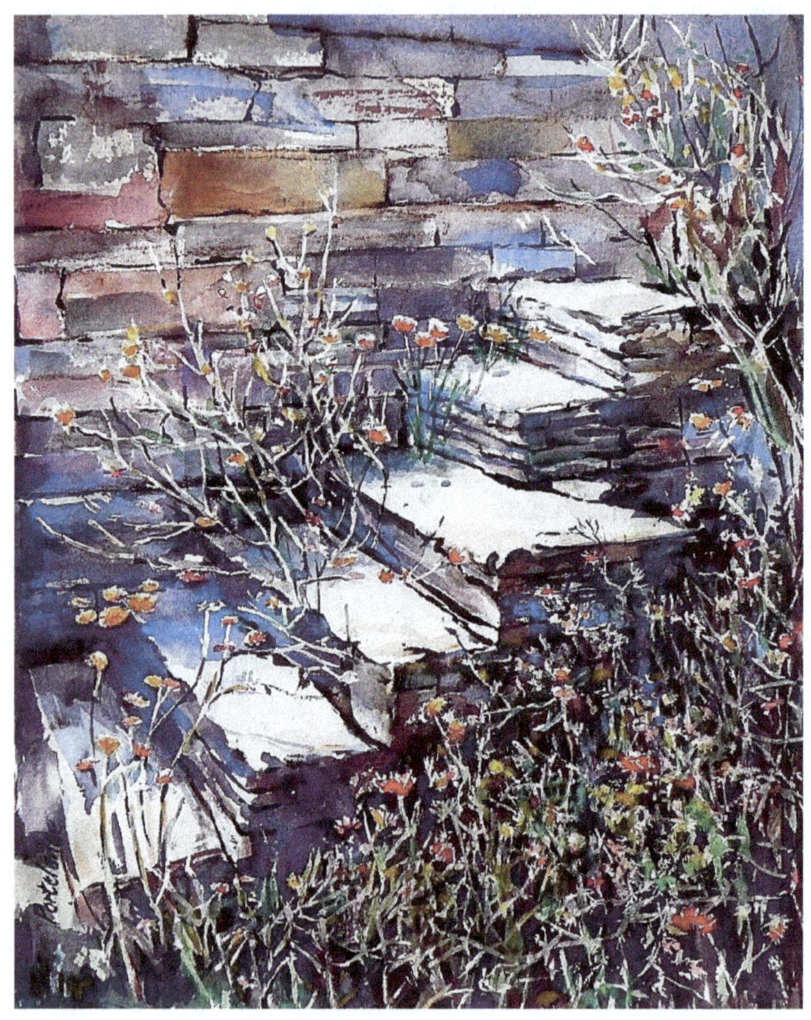

Stairway to the Gods

And now,
The final journey begins.
I walk through pale powdered petals
Travelling with ghosts from my past
And familiar angels
On the stairway to the Gods

Under a metallic translucent sky
The coo of a dove drifts
On the whisper of the waves.
Beneath a luminous sun
I can see clearly now.
Through the years of indecision,
The moments of indiscretion,
Faulty choices, wasted days and nights;
But my compass point has remained magnetized
Drawing me unwittingly, yet relentlessly, to my destiny.

Through heartache and tears,
Laughter and smiles,
Success and failures,
From the depths of despair to the heights of success
Coming full circle and repeating again.
Karma and the wheels of fate
Lead me onto the stairway to the Gods.

At the last steps, weary and fragile
I am lifted by a flurry of wings
From the veiled mists of life
Where I rest in the arms of the angels
As the final journey ends.

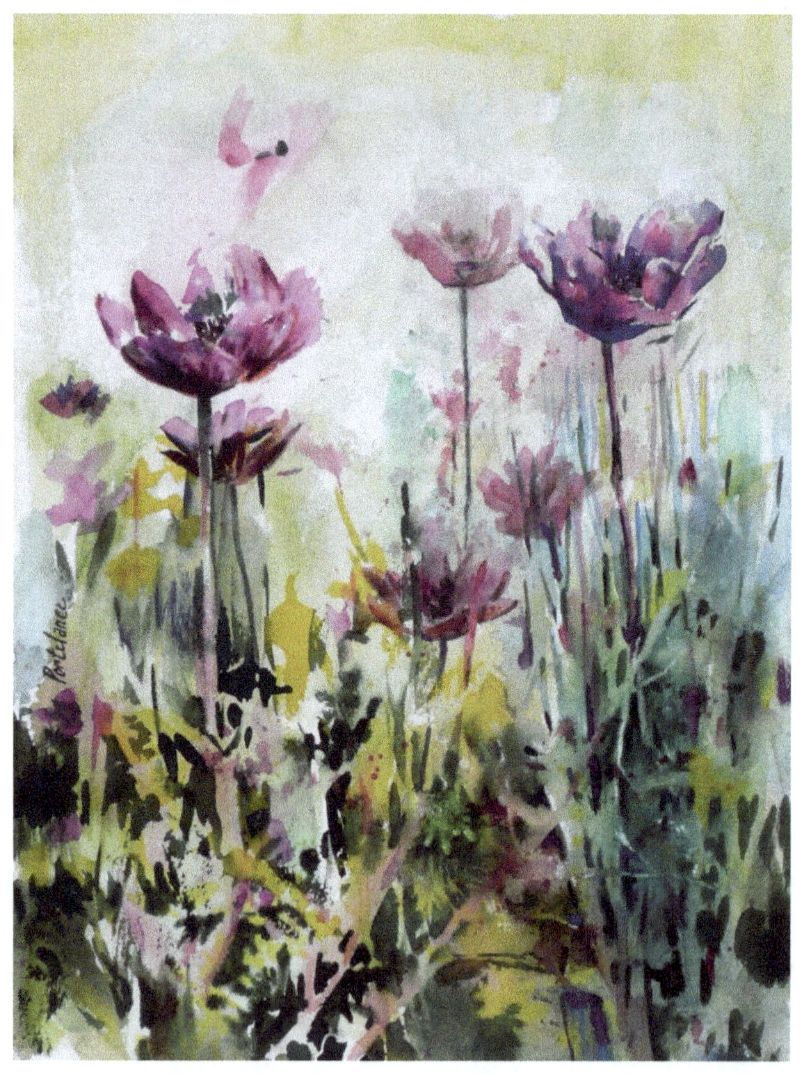

Wildflowers

The sun glittered overhead.
And my mind peeled into segments
Of purple, yellow, green and blue,
Drifting me casually back
On rivers of mirrored diamonds,
To the inception of the wildflowers

A sky heart
Was beating and pounding
In harmony with my heart
And the satin echoes of the wind.

This moment, This sky heart,
These wildflowers,
Beneath the glittering sun overhead,
Twist at the windmills in my mind.
I see my name pulsating
On the walls, floor and ceiling.
Now I can feel it....
The sky heart beating In unison with mine.

As we become one
With the glittering sun overhead
The wildflowers whisper,
Through damp petal flutes.
A world weariness envelops me.

Twilight yawns,
I lay down in nature's lap,
Safe within the wildflowers keep.

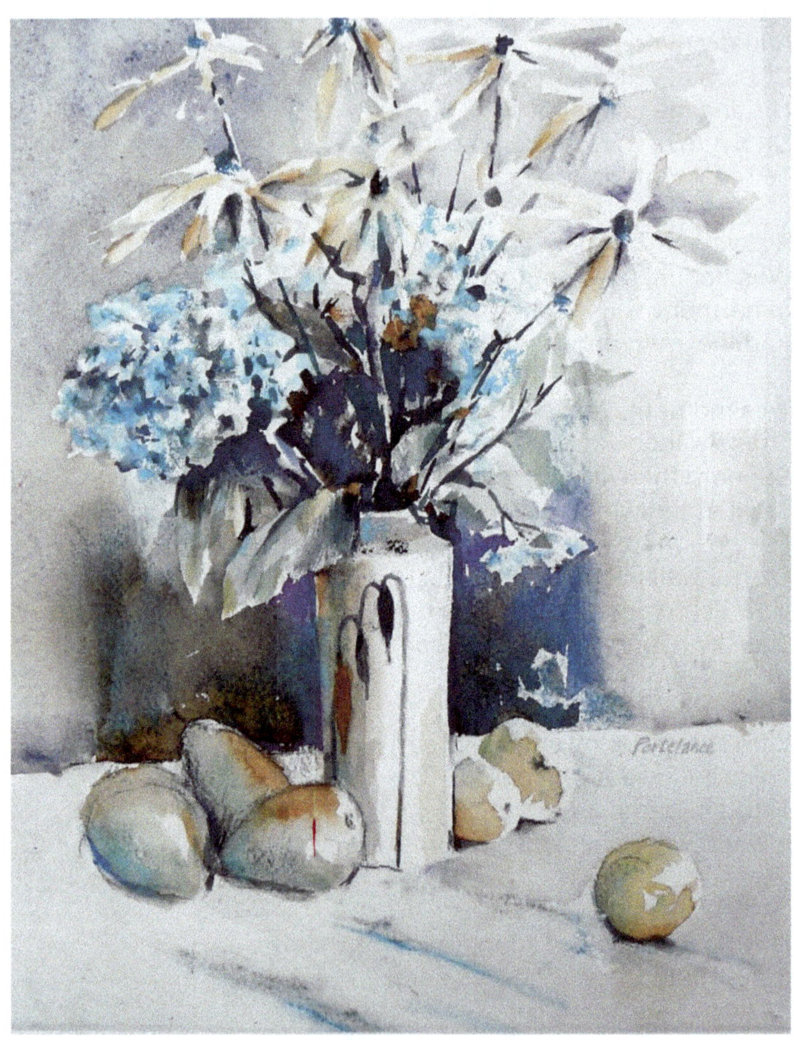

Gleaming

This dream...

A wet, gleaming, intrinsic beauty,
Water streaked with kisses,
Dances like diamonds on the surface of this dream;

A mirror shining silver moments to gold,
Polishing dust into splendor,
Jewels a wish
To make it come true.

Wishes become horses
Riding the winds of change
          Into the eye
Of this vivid needlepoint dream.

It's gleaming so bright.
I'm blinded by its light,
But sight is no longer required.
All that's required is the dream.

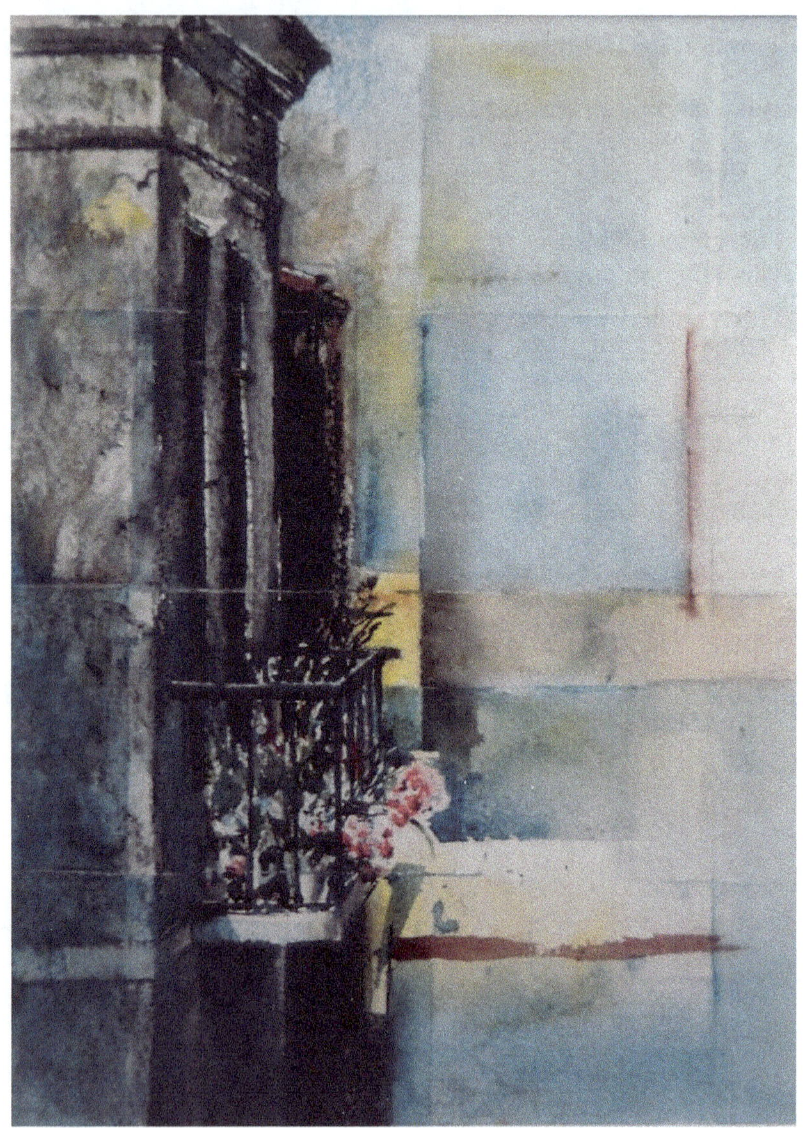

Lisbon

The last streaks of sunlight
Flex through the weary streets.
          Silence,
Prevalent in the still of approaching night,
As it weaves its thick black threads
Through the last remnants of twilight.

The days fly by Like painted kites
Amidst a backdrop
Of church bells and laughter,
Pealing in harmony
Through this slice of life,
Alive with easy living.

Nights parade by
In a cavalcade of champagne moments
And strawberry wine kisses,
Embracing the heart of the city,
Molding it into the essence of enchantment.

A lemon sun bakes the day's griddle.
A pearl moon waxes the evening horizon.
Stars sequin the overhead ebony tapestry.

Time stands still
Then slowly disappears
Down eternity's rabbit hole;

  And somehow,
Summer never ends
    In Lisbon.

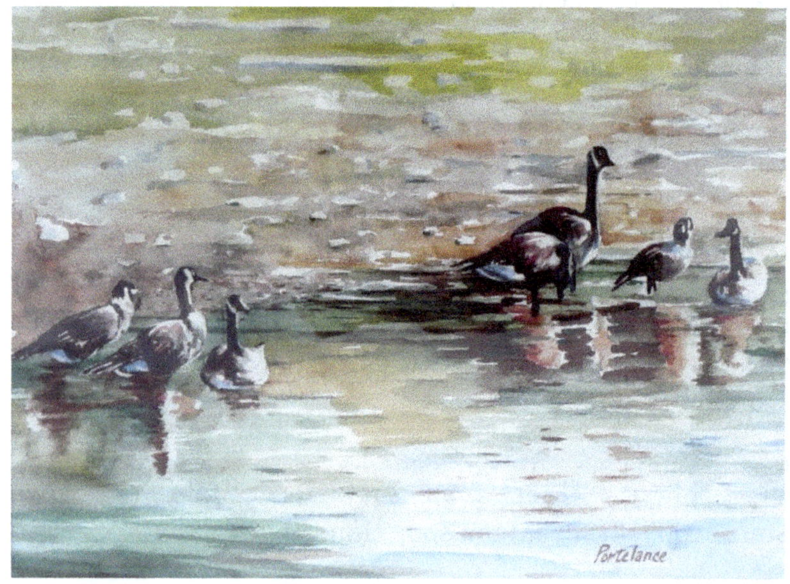

Splash

A splash
Of muted green,
Pale coral and rustic rose;
Shiny blue water and white foam
Surround the wading ducks.

It's a gentle kind of day,
With shot silk overtones,
Streaked onto a renaissance waterscape.

Inside this surreal moment
Nature's velvet underside reveals itself
In a wizardry of living colours.

All cares disappear
As we watch the ducks
Wading, splashing;
We so aware of them,
They so oblivious to us.

It's a lazy kind of day
We kick back our heels,
And rest in this moment.

A slice of nature,
A splash of colour
Dripping gentle beauty
Onto life's bland canvas.

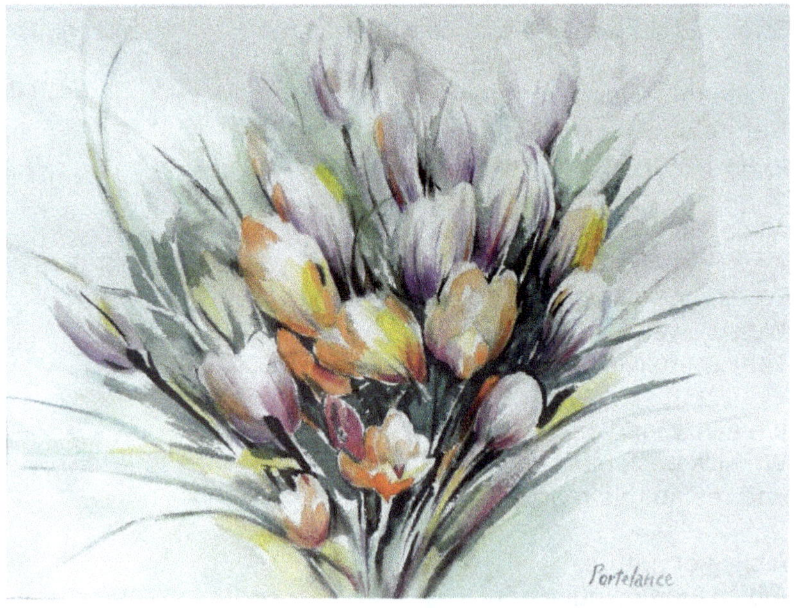
Portelance

Timeless

The bouquet whispers
In captivating tones.
I sit in silence and reverence.
My mind weaves a brand new story
From a thread of feathered gauze
Shed from an angels' wing.

Winding through a myriad
Of damp petal flutes
And vivid colours,
I search tirelessly
For the perfect pink and white moment.

In the whisper of a steamy hush
I dream of cherry blossom days,
Summer raindrops
And cloudless skies.

The petals touch their silky lips
To my cheek
In a tender springtime kiss
As the moment arrives.

Dreaming, Suspended,
Inside this captured and coveted
Pink and white moment,
I become
Timeless.

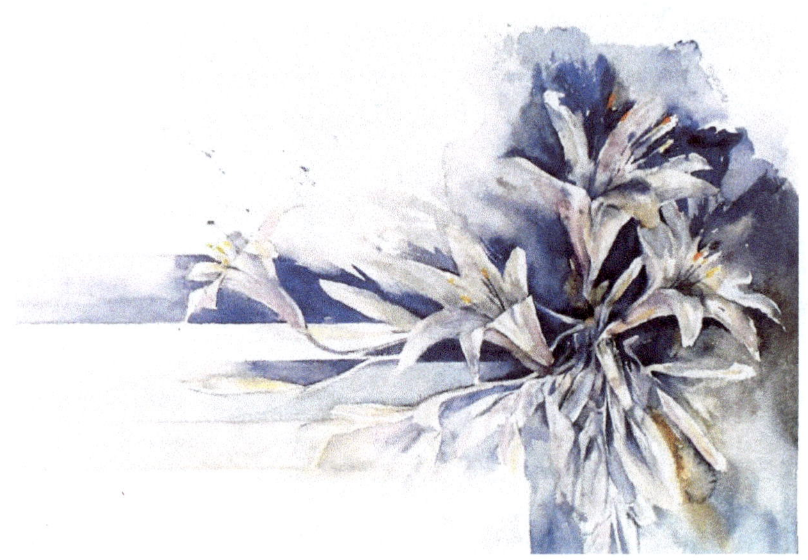

Greek Lilies

Through a super-imposed shadow
Of an ancient crumbled past,
A ghostly god from antiquity
Peeks surreptitiously
Through the fine layered atmosphere,
Shining the pastel lilies;
Melding them into the rich indigo shade
Of a long lost Parthenon era.

An rock hewn Chieftain's sculpted crown,
Below the ghostly godhead
Decorates a worn out moccasin
That's left its imprint in another space,
As if time had overlapping dimensions,
Rectangles and squares to merge into.

      White water,
       White sky,
Separated by the indigo italics
Of a long lost language,
Have rendered us directionless.

We are drifters riding
In chauffeur driven dreams,
Residing on shaky layers of refuted reality.
Chasing ourselves to catch up to our shadows,
    We have no time
To stop and smell the flowers;

But still, the Greek lilies bloom...
    Despite our inattention.

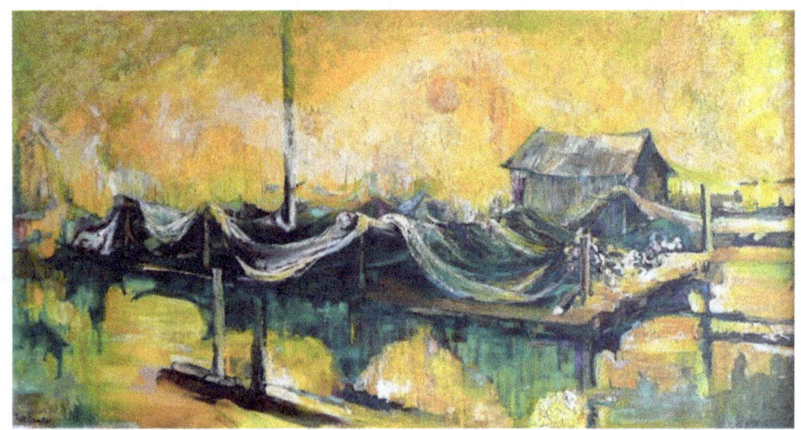

The Nets

A pale orange sun peeks
Through a mottled ochre
And talcum dusted sky
Onto the damp, briny
Spread-eagled nets
Reflecting in water
That looks like sky.

Nets,
Shore bound,
Languish in the sun.

Now...
The fish run free and easy,
Gliding beneath the waves,
Unobstructed by the nets.

The threat of the nets
Lies dormant,
Baking beneath
An egg splattered sky;
And every night,
Under a waning moon,
The ocean mixes
With tears of the sea
As the nets fall asleep.

Tomorrow,
Dawn will slice the sky
And crack open a new egg.
The nets will rise up,
Drier than the sun,
Ready to dive
Into the tears of the sea.

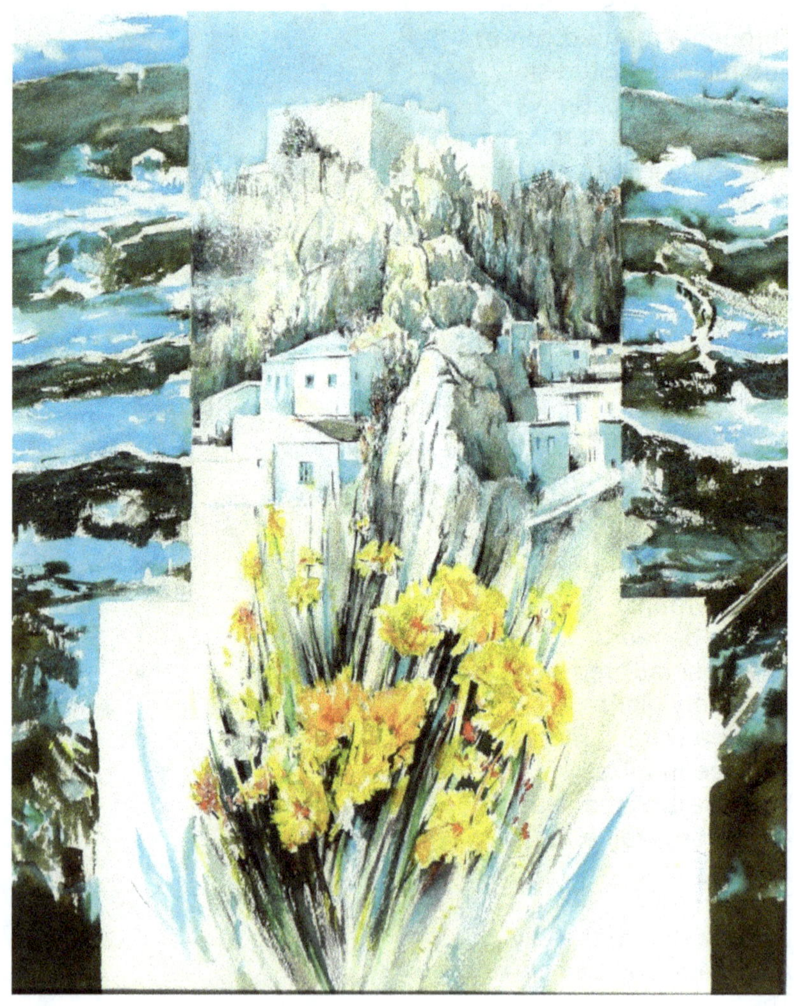

Greek Fantasy

The blue and white city
Of levels and waters,
Beneath the shadows
In a floral spray of light,
Spreads a magical silence
Across a damp petal sky,
Spilling yellows and golds,
Oranges and reds of glorious scent.

A sensuous aromatic breeze
Drifts into the lap of a mystic valley
That's lain hidden for eras and eons.

In a faraway swirling dream
A pale ghostly figure stirs.
Pan, the God of shepherds and flocks,
Wakes from eternal slumber.
In the mountains of the wild
He wanders down from the hills
Into the sacred realm of blue waters.

Playing rustic music
On his pan-pipes,
He scales the levels
And walks on the waters
In the city of blue and white,
Beneath the shadows of light.

He weaves his hypnotic spell
In moving majestic melody
And love comes tumbling down
In glorious passionate images
Of mystery and Greek fantasy.

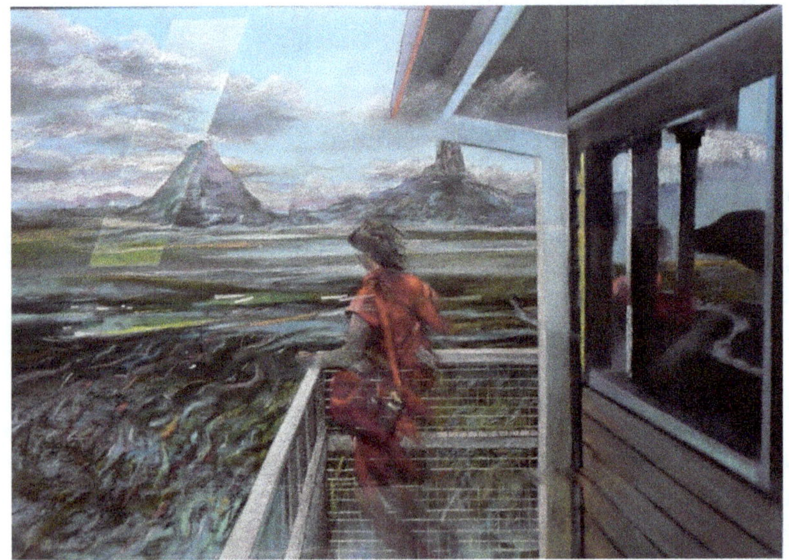

Time at Glass House Mountains

Time at Glasshouse Mountains
Dimensionalizes in slow motion fade out,
Braiding past, present and future,
Blending the real and illusion,
Bending the hands of time
Into quantum blue moments;
Running rampant,
Crashing into a talcum powder sky
Inside the fabric of forever.

And then,
Brilliant splashes of lilac and pink
Roll the sky curtains aside;
Angels smiling,
Teeth gleaming,
Chew the blue notes
Into transcendental muon dust.

These angels,
Billowing like ivory sky boats
On a metallic inverse sea,
Paint this dimensionalized world
A glossier tint of blue.

Blue turns to raw, red, naked notes
That mist over, rain down,
Nestle into the shifting atmosphere
And permeate the fabric of forever,
Forever.

Reality dimensionalizes in slow motion fade-out.
Time at Glass House Mountains
Ceases to exist.

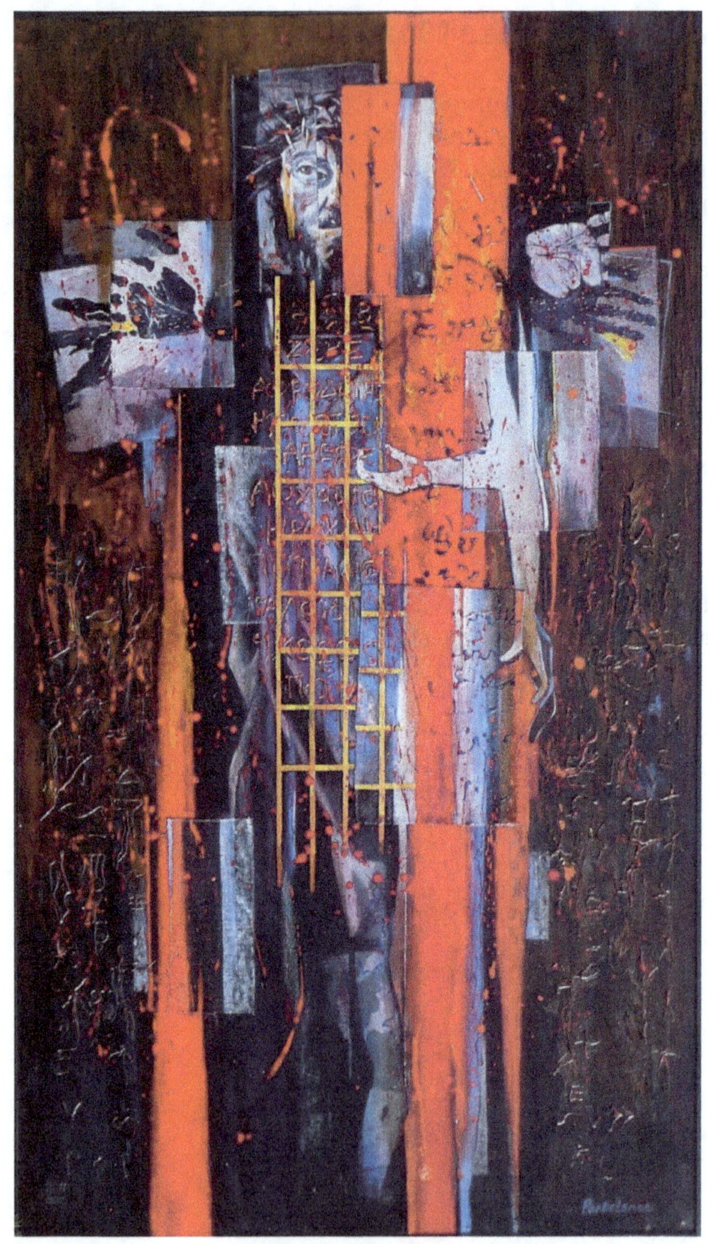

The Artist as a Saviour –
The Saviour as an Artist

The artist as a Saviour, in splashes of red and gold,
Exchanges time and space with the Saviour as an artist.
Slipping through a clear blue window in the blood, Abstractions of
emotion wound the atmosphere
And paint laments across the face of destiny.

There is a hollow, sorrowful, unuttered moan
Trapped in the throat of sacrosanct knowledge.
This scathing travesty of mind, matter and spirit
Unwraps, disrobes, and displays a tainted tribulation
Of decades and centuries past and the sin we cannot hide.
A silent visual recording of the naked lamb laid slain
Innocence forever lost, drowned in the tears of time.

In the ethereal exchange of artist and Saviour,
Blood on the brush and the brushing of blood,
A sacred grace creeps through blood, sweat and tears
Spilled from the fingerprints of eternal redemption.

An albatross shadow unwittingly crosses an angel's face. Scarlet
teardrops, stained and scarred with innocent blood Fall from
Heaven's soul and shake the foundations of hell
For the sake of the Saviour, the artist, mankind.

Wrapped in a silent prayer, and kissed by an angel's lips
The painter and the painting are interlaced forever:
"The artist as a Saviour - The Saviour as an artist"

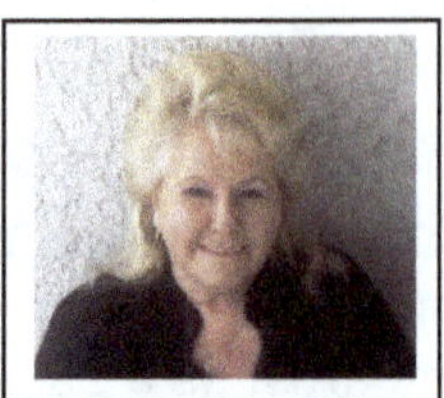

CANDICE JAMES
Poet Laureate (2010 – 2016)
City of New Westminster, BC CANADA
appointed Poet Laureate Emerita
by City Council Nov 2016

Candice James is Founder of Royal City Literary Arts Society,
full member of The League of Canadian Poets, Honorary Professor
International Arts Academy (Greece); Board Advisor Muse-Int.
Journal of Poetry (India); Past President of the Federation of
British Columbia Writers, Past Director of SpoCan, Past President of
Slam Central, creator of series "Poetic Justice"; "Poetry in the Park"
and "Slam Central;

She is recipient of the following awards "Chamber of Commerce
Bernie Legge Artist of year"; Pandora's Collective "Citizen of Year"
Writers International Network "Distinguished Poet"; "Woman of
Prestige" Pentasi B Poetry Conference, Manila, Philippines
and she has judged "Fred Cogswell Award for Excellence in Poetry";
The League of Canadian Poets "Jessamy Stursberg Canadian Youth
Poet Award" and "Pat Lowther Memorial Award".

Candice has featured on "Wax Poetic", "World Poetry Café", and
"Story Time". She has led workshops and been keynote speaker,
at "Word on the Street"; Black Dot Cultural Collective";"Write
on The Beach" and "Lit Fest New West". She has been featured
at Crossroads Hospice Donors' Dinners and New Westminster
Hospice Society "Dialogues on Death and Dying" reading from her
book "Behind the One-Way Mirror" 2023. Her poetry has
appeared in a variety of local and international magazines, e-zines
and newspapers. She has led online forums, reviewed books and
written prefaces for authors and poets internationally and hosted
National Poetry month for the League of Canadian Poets 6 times.

She is the Author of 25 poetry books, The first one:
        "A SPLIT IN THE WATER" - Fiddlehead Poetry Books 1979;
the latest one   "DEEP BLUE SILENCE" Silver Bow Publishing 2024

For Further information visit www.candicejames.com

DON PORTELANCE
Artist

Don Portelance was born and raised in Vancouver, Br[itish Columbia].
He has juried exhibits, and led art conferences and workshops in
Canada, the U.S.A. and Australia. Don has taken part in hundreds of
solo and group exhibitions in China, Japan and Korea.

He has received many awards, notably the first Tri-Cities "Excellence
in the Arts Award", and the Tri-Cities Chamber of Commerce "Arts
and Entertainment Personality of the Year". He founded Coquitlam
Fine Arts Council, and was instrumental in establishing Place des Arts
arts school.

Throughout a lifetime of producing contemporary original paintings he
has found himself drawn to two themes:

One theme, based on observation, is usually inspired by, or produced
while traveling locally and globally; a common theme is the desire to
capture a quality of light and explore expressive realism. A 2nd theme
is based on ideas, and often tends to be more abstract as he attempts
to examine through symbols, the encounter of deeply held cultural
beliefs with new scientific data related to those beliefs.

Don Portelance website
http://portelancestudios.com

Don Portelance Facebook Page
http://www.facebook.com/donportelanceartist

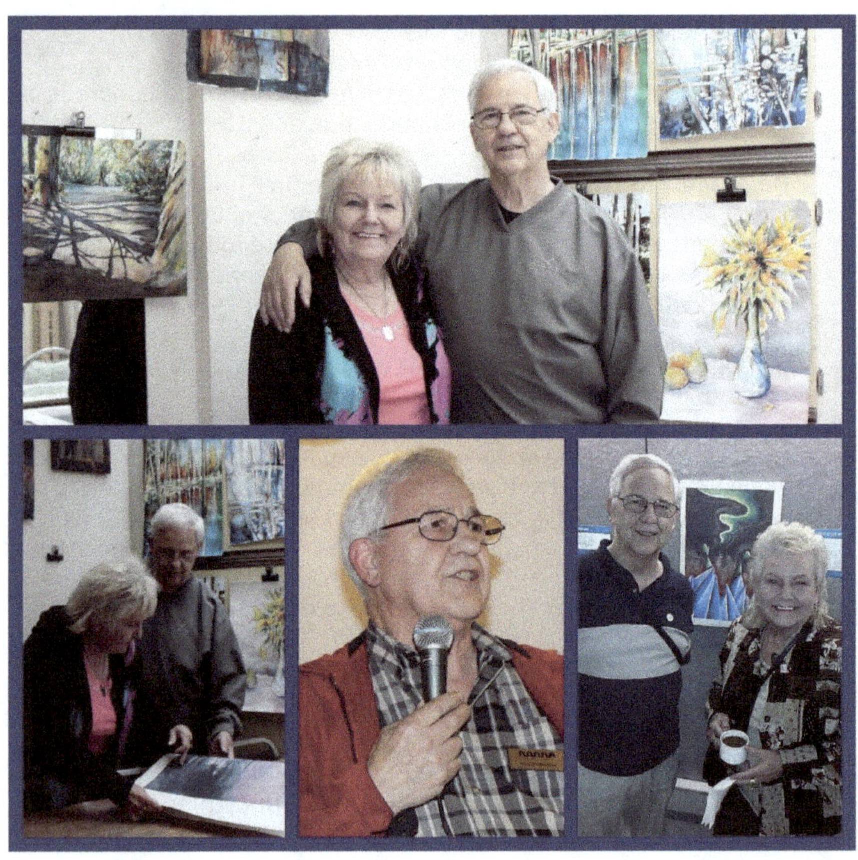